PUT MORE MONEY IN YOUR POCKET!

Buying or selling a business can be a lucrative but risky transaction –it's all too easy to sell yourself short or to overpay as a buyer. If you want to avoid the costly mistakes that many business owners make in buying and selling companies, this book is for you! It provides valuable guidance on how to negotiate your deal, and how to walk away from the table with more money in your pocket.

A popular maxim says that average people learn from their own mistakes, stupid people repeat their mistakes, and brilliant people learn from the mistakes and successes of others. This book is designed to nudge you toward the brilliant category among business owners who buy and sell privately-held companies. Even if you hire a seasoned team of M&A professionals to guide you (highly recommended) through your deal, the insights in this book could be worth millions of dollars to you!

The owners of most businesses buy or sell a company once in their lifetime. However, on the other side of the table in the transaction may be an unscrupulous or unsophisticated buyer/seller. This book will help you even the odds by giving you the knowledge to sidestep the pitfalls of M&A transactions.

Too many business owners get caught in the day-to-day minutia of managing their company and have few options when the opportunity comes to buy another company or to sell theirs. Most don't realize that it often takes two years or longer to prepare a company to be sold, and about a year to get ready to buy a company. Furthermore, it's likely to take six to nine months more to close the deal. This book will help you shorten the time—and get it right the first time!

D0596452

ABOUT THE AUTHORS

Stuart Sorkin and Dick Stieglitz met at a weekend retreat for a men's group called the Mankind Project (MKP). It didn't take long to discover they had common business interests and, more importantly, shared business values. After the weekend, they met for lunch to explore opportunities and to begin planning Dick's exit from the company that he had founded 20 years earlier. Dick's objectives were vague, but he knew he wanted to pass part of the proceeds from the sale of his company to his heirs. Stuart suggested that Dick transfer some of his stock to a family trust in return for a second-to-die annuity. Stuart prepared trust documents, served as interim trustee, and represented the trust in negotiations. After the deal closed, Dick and Stuart began collaborating to help business owners buy other companies or prepare their company to be sold. This book is based on their M&A experiences and their interviews with business owners and other M&A professionals.

DICK STIEGLITZ, PHD

Dick Stieglitz has experienced the spectrum of M&A transactions. He was a manager in a company that was sold, was involved in transactions to buy companies, and built and sold his own company for what experts called a top multiple. Since he sold his company, Dick has consulted with CEOs who are building their companies through organic growth and acquisitions or are grooming it to be sold. Dick earned a PhD in Nuclear Engineering at Rensselear Polytechnic Institute, and served ten years refueling submarines as a naval officer. After leaving the Navy, he was Vice President in a software firm and Director of Consulting for an aerospace company. In 1984, Dick began his company and pioneered the Integrated Change Management (ICM) methodology. His earlier book, *Taming the Dragons of Change in Business*, is based on 30 years experience in helping business and government executives achieve positive organizational change.

STUART SORKIN, JD, LL.M, CPA

Stuart Sorkin has represented buyers and sellers in M&A transactions for more than 25 years. He has participated in transactions involving publicly-traded companies, but mostly he helps owners of privately-held companies buy and sell businesses. He began his career working in the tax department of an international accounting firm, and moved to the national tax office of another international accounting firm where he consulted with their local offices on M&A transactions. For the past 20 years, Stuart has worked for various law firms where he specialized in M&A transactions, asset protection, and estate planning. Stuart earned a JD from the University of Miami Law School and an LL.M at Georgetown University Law Center, and is also a Certified Public Accountant.

EXPENSIVE MISTAKES WHEN BUYING & SELLING COMPANIES

IF YOU PLAN TO BUY OR SELL A PRIVATELY-HELD
BUSINESS, THIS BOOK COULD BE WORTH
MILLIONS OF DOLLARS TO YOU!

EXPENSIVE MISTAKES

WHEN BUYING & SELLING COMPANIES

...AND HOW TO AVOID THEM IN YOUR DEALS

Richard G. Stieglitz, PhD
Stuart H. Sorkin, JD, LL.M, CPA

Potomac, Maryland

Acuity Publishing
9812 Falls Road #114-157
Potomac, Maryland 20854-3863
301-365-9031, Fax: 301-365-9041
Info@AcuityPublishing.Com

Disclaimer

This publication is designed to educate and provide general information regarding the subject matter covered. The reader is encouraged to consult with his or her own advisors regarding specific situations. While the authors have take reasonable precautions in the preparation of this book and believe the facts presented within the book are accurate, neither the publisher nor the authors assume any responsibility for errors or omissions. The authors and publisher specifically disclaim any liability resulting from the use or application of the information contained in this book. This book was written to introduce business owners to the motivations, complexities, and processes involved in buying or selling a privately-held business. The book is not a substitute for competent strategic, legal, and financial advisors for those who are contemplating, planning, or executing an acquisition or sale transaction.

Publisher's Cataloging-In-Publication

Stieglitz, Richard G.

Expensive mistakes when buying & selling companies : and how to avoid them in your deals / Richard G. Stieglitz, Stuart H. Sorkin. --
1st ed. -- Potomac, MD : Acuity Publishing, c2010.

p. ; cm.

ISBN: 978-0-9820500-6-4

1. Business enterprises--Purchasing. 2. Sale of business enterprises. I. Sorkin, Stuart H. II. Title.

HD1393.25 .S75 2010   2009939983
658.16--dc22   1001

Printed in the United States of America.

Cover and book design: Patricia Bacall

This book is dedicated to entrepreneurs who have taken the plunge to start their own privately-held businesses. We admire the courage, the creativity, and the dedication it takes to achieve success.

Other Books by Dick Stieglitz

ON CHANGES IN THE WORLD OF BUSINESS:

Taming the Dragons of Change in Business

How to Thrive, Not Just Survive, in
a Rapidly Changing Global Economy

ON PERSONAL CHANGE:

Taming the Dragons of Change

10 Tips For Achieving Happiness & Success
When Everything Around You Is Changing

CONTENTS

FOREWORD

By Jeff Copeland, CEO, immixGroup Inc.

Mergers and acquisitions (M&A) are an emotional roller coaster for anyone who hasn't navigated the process several times. The M&A process of buying, selling, and integrating companies consumes an enormous amount of executive time. Even for a professionally managed and well-financed company, the best-planned acquisitions can be costly and stretch critical resources. The more you know about the M&A process—its costs and benefits—the more likely you are to have a successful transaction.

If you are contemplating an M&A transaction, whether as a buyer or a seller, it can take a year or longer to prepare a company to be sold or to find a good acquisition candidate. If you haven't been preparing for such a transaction in advance, you probably will not be ready to pursue the perfect acquisition target when it hits the market, or to walk away with top dollar when a buyer with deep pockets expresses a strong interest in your company.

I wish I had known more about M&A transactions before my company's first few acquisitions. I learned about M&A the hard way: through trial and error. If I knew then what I now know after living through some difficult learning experiences, I'm confident our acquisitions would have been less costly and more efficient. I certainly would have lost less sleep worrying that I was paying too much, that the deal was going to fall apart, or that it was just the wrong thing to do from a strategic or tactical perspective. Fortunately, most of the transactions have worked out well for my company and for me.

To substantially improve the odds of making a successful acquisition, an entrepreneur needs the counsel of professionals who have years of experience and the hard-won knowledge gained from numerous transactions. You may be a successful entrepreneur who runs a very profitable business. This does not mean, however, that you have the expertise required to determine the right criteria to locate the best acquisition targets. It does not guarantee that you will know how to negotiate and close the deal, or how to best merge a new company's business and personnel into your current operations and corporate culture. These issues require a set of skills and experience that you and your management team may not currently possess.

For these reasons, adding experts like Stuart and Dick to your team is the most effective way to prepare for and complete a successful acquisition. They were critical to our process. They developed alternative deal structures and helped us decide which to implement. They knew how to determine the value of a target, negotiate a fair price, and arrange financing. They provided post-closing advice on merging operations to extract the highest value.

Stuart and Dick understood the pitfalls. They helped us avoid costly mistakes, and led me through the process of making the right decisions. In one instance, this meant the best decision was walking away from what would have likely become a bad acquisition.

This book is a valuable resource—and a fascinating read—for anyone who owns a business, plans to sell or buy a business, or is a professional (such as a lawyer, broker, or accountant) who advises buyers and sellers. After reading this book, you will see that M&A deals are as much art as science, and you will know what to expect and what not to expect. That knowledge alone will improve the odds that your M&A transaction will close, meet your expectations, and produce profitable results.

BEGIN WITH THE END IN MIND

A successful acquisition or sale is created three times: first in your imagination as a possibility, second in your plans as an objective, and third in reality as the result of your actions.

A popular maxim says that average people learn from their mistakes, stupid people repeat their mistakes, and brilliant people learn from the mistakes and successes of others. This book will nudge you toward the brilliant category among entrepreneurs who buy and sell privately-held companies. Even if you hire a seasoned team of merger and acquisition (M&A) professionals to guide you (a step we recommend highly), the insights in this book can be worth millions of dollars.

One of the basic mistakes that many business owners make is they don't have an exit plan—they don't begin and run their companies with the end (their exit) in mind. For most of the twenty-two years that Dick Stieglitz (co-author of this book) owned his company, he lacked an exit strategy. He simply had a sweet dream that someday he would sell the company and live happily ever after like he saw other owners do. If you founded a company or own a share of a privately-held company, this book will help turn your sweetest dreams into reality: growing by buying other companies and eventually selling your company. This concept will help you begin with the end in mind.

Dick's first exposure to M&A transactions came a few years after he started his own company. He entered the government services industry in 1976 after leaving the Navy. His employer was very successful until a start-up firm called Advanced Technology (*AdTech*) came along and kicked butt in competitions during the Reagan defense buildup. They won contracts for Dick's Marine Corps tasks and his work at a Navy lab—contracts that his company had held for years. In 1984, Dick left to start his own company and forgot about *AdTech*.

In 1988, however, the government services industry was jolted by the news that Black & Decker had purchased *AdTech* for $140 million. The transaction was curious in two ways: why would the owners sell such a profitable business, and why would a publicly-traded company pay so much for a company that was outside their mainstream? In any case, the founders of *AdTech* walked away with about $30 million each—not bad for a company started in 1976! Dick wondered: "*Wow, how did they get so much cash? I want to do that!*" At the time, his company had a few million dollars in revenue, but thoughts of selling it became a dream. Unfortunately, for years it was just a sugar-plum-fairy dream. Dick was fascinated by new technologies but ignorant about how to use them to build a sellable business.

When he founded the company in 1984, he specialized in submarine engineering and logistics. After all, that was where he had spent most of his life building relationships. His company did cool jobs and made a tidy profit. They designed a computer application to manage replaceable equipments, and helped to implement a phototonics mast that eliminated periscopes in combat situations. The mast appeared to be garbage floating on the ocean, but it was tethered to the submarine and was full of electronics for counter-measures, communications, and optics. They also worked on what at the time was a top-secret project for noise cancellation. Today, you can find the technology in Bose earphones.

Then in 1989, the Berlin Wall fell and the country stopped building submarines. The program that funded his bread-and-butter projects was cut from twenty-nine ships to three. At the time, his annual revenue was about $4 million. But, one by one, Dick's projects ended and there were no new contracts. He was devastated. It looked like the end of the line for his company and his dream to sell it for a mountain of cash.

But being tenacious, Dick rebuilt the company in the early 1990s into an information technology firm with web development and computer network skills. Again, he focused on technology rather than on building a sellable company. The submarine engineers left the company and were replaced by IT specialists. Things turned around. His revenue doubled from what it was when he focused on submarine technologies.

Then, in 2000, the Navy awarded the $8 billion Navy-Marine Corps Intranet contract to Electronic Data Systems to maintain its shore-based computer systems and networks. Once again, Dick's contract options weren't renewed. Revenue was cut in half, and he suffered through his first-ever annual loss. Most of the IT specialists left for greener pastures. The company was on life support—but then he had an epiphany.

Twice he had bet his company's future on a technology, ignoring the fact that technologies have short commercial lives. So he re-branded the company around change. The nature of the change made no difference. A new supply chain, an organizational consolidation, an outsourcing, or a new web application were all the same. His company pioneered the Integrated Change Management (ICM) methodology, and trained its consultants to help clients anticipate and use change to their advantage. The company competed favorably versus elite federal suppliers like Accenture and IBM by showing clients that the success of their business change depended on how people reacted to change, not on the bells and whistles designed into their new computer systems.

It worked! That growth strategy was sustainable. Dick's company won multi-year contracts, built a strong management team, documented processes, and accurately projected future revenue and profits. In short, Dick did the things that make a company valuable to buyers. Revenue grew at a compounded annual growth rate (CAGR) of 20 percent until the company was sold in 2006. It was a robust M&A market in which to sell a company, especially one focused on federal contracts.

Relative to building a sellable business, Dick essentially wasted the first 18 years of his company's existence. Like many entrepreneurs, he was a perpetual motion *DO-DO* machine. He rushed through meetings, e-mails, and decisions trying to finish everything on his *things-to-do* list. He read time-management books and used software tools to help him *DO* tasks more efficiently so he could *DO* more. But getting more done wasn't his biggest challenge. His real problem was that he wasn't doing the right things to increase the value of his company.

Dick's journey toward a lucrative M&A transaction began when he first realized his company was not ready to be sold and took action to make it attractive to buyers. He determined how large the company had to be to satisfy his financial needs (price being a multiple of revenue and profits) and implemented a strategy to reach that size. He strengthened the management team by training a new president and CFO from inside the company, and hired a vice president of sales and marketing. He also had advisors, the Board of Directors being among the most valuable, that helped him with business development and financial management strategies. The Board didn't depend on Dick, so they could challenge him with frank advice. In addition, Stuart Sorkin (co-author of this book) made it clear that Dick needed a financial plan to minimize tax consequences of the sale, to manage the sale proceeds, and to protect the after-tax proceeds from estate taxes and creditors.

When Dick sold the company in late 2006, favorable external factors (e.g., top multipliers and loose underwriting standards) had stimulated intense M&A activity. Announcements of billion-dollar deals appeared often in newspapers. In the mid-market where companies like Dick's were sold, banks were eager to approve loans to buy companies.

What a difference a year can make. When the credit market collapsed and private equity firms went into hibernation in 2008, M&A deals fell 30 percent according to Dealogic, a New York research firm. Buyers couldn't get financing under the same favorable terms as before. Pricing multiples held steady, but both strategic and financial buyers were only interested in companies with proven revenue models, marketable services and products, steady cash flow, a clearly identifiable and stable customer base, and a seasoned executive team.

Starting in 2008, several trillion dollars in federal bailouts, stimulus packages, and deficit budgets pushed the economy toward recovery. But the M&A market had changed. Industry consolidations continued, but at a slower pace. Buyers still used M&A transactions to build market share and core capabilities, but they did deals by leveraging their balance sheets instead of using debt. While credit markets often ebb and flow, it is safe to assume buyers will be interested in acquiring businesses in growth industries with a strong management team. Entrepreneurs who start or grow companies would be wise to choose markets that buyers will value when it comes time to exit. Companies in growth areas like energy, law enforcement, health care, education, and information technology will find market conditions that are favorable.

The value of a company typically is a multiple of its revenue and its earnings before income tax, depreciation, and amortization (EBITDA). The range of multiples is determined by the industry, but factors under a business owner's control will influence whether the multiple is at the top or bottom of the range. For example, in government services, buyers place a high value on multi-year contracts and security clearances. When Dick consults with CEOs to increase the value of their company, he uses a list of 17 factors that increase value (see Appendix). Knowing these factors, it is often possible for an owner to increase the company's value by 20 percent or more simply by making the company more attractive in those areas. On the other hand, buyers can use the 17 factors to define criteria for selecting acquisition targets, and doing due diligence to quantify the real strategic value of the target company.

Successful M&A transactions are win-win events that produce value for both buyer and seller. A mistake by either side can be costly for the other. The 57 mistakes described in this book address best practices on both sides of a transaction, so they will be valuable regardless of which side you are on. M&A transactions are like Heinz-57 sauces: There is a variety of spicy and expensive mistakes to make! Our experience and the consensus of the experts we interviewed show that roughly:

- One in ten preliminary discussions between a qualified buyer and a willing seller leads to a signed Letter of Intent (LOI)
- Sixty percent of the signed LOIs actually close (the experts' experiences varied between 40 and 80 percent)
- Transactions (even those that don't close) can easily cost $20,000 or more (often a lot more) in professional fees
- Two-thirds of the closed transactions produce the expected value, which is a higher percentage than for publicly-traded companies!

The experts all agree on the importance of starting early to prepare for and preserve options for selling or buying a company. Since M&A markets shift constantly, it's important to be ready to do a deal when an opportunity appears. Reading this book is part of that preparation.

This book is mainly for business owners who are selling a company, but it is also valuable for entrepreneurs who would rather buy a business than start one, and business owners who plan to grow their companies through acquisitions. For most people, buying or selling a company is a once-in-a-lifetime deal. But the person on the other side of the table may represent a firm or equity investor who buys and sells several companies a year. You might even be dealing with an unethical or unscrupulous person. This book evens the odds by helping you understand the steps in the M&A process and the hazards involved in each step.

Whether you are the buyer or seller in a transaction, it is vital that you understand the other side. That's why Chapters 1 and 2 discuss preparations from the view of the seller and buyer, respectively; and Chapters 3 and 4 discuss the flow of the deal from the two perspectives. Of course, post-closing integration (Chapter 5) is where the two entities merge. While buyer and seller both are concerned about price and other terms and conditions, the buyer is most concerned about the post-deal results and potential pitfalls in integration. Sellers are concerned about integration only when earn-outs are part of the purchase price, or if they will work for the merged company for an extended period of time.

About half of the stories in this book are about deals where Stuart or Dick were involved as a participant, consultant, or legal counsel. In all cases, the business that was sold was privately-held. Other stories are from entrepreneurs who purchased and sold companies; professionals whose full-time job is to acquire companies; and brokers, accountants, and lawyers who assist in M&A transactions. We promised our clients and contributors that we would respect their privacy, so names are not used in the stories. In some cases, peripheral details about the deal and the industry were omitted or adjusted for that reason.

Stuart and Dick consider it to be a weighty responsibility and a great privilege to help business owners complete M&A transactions. We believe that by sharing our knowledge, we can expedite deals in the small and mid-market. Besides, working with buyers and sellers who understand M&A processes makes our job easier and produces better results for everyone. That's why we wrote this book! So as you begin to read it, keep in mind the end result you want to achieve.

CHAPTER ONE

PREPARING FOR A DEAL AS THE SELLER

The quality and timeliness of preparations for selling your company will be a major factor in the price you eventually receive when you sell it.

Regardless of when you think you might offer your business for sale, start preparing today for that transaction. Ideally, you began developing an exit strategy when you started the company and have used that strategy in making decisions. Generally, owners think about selling their business years before an exit but take few, if any, actions to build its value. For example, they may talk about a sale that coincides with a retirement date years in the future, but as the adage says, "*talk is cheap*." Unfortunately, you may suddenly find yourself with an urgent need to sell your business because of a personal matter. Failure to prepare could cost you millions because your business won't be ready when you want or need to sell it.

Dick started his company in 1984 and grew it to nearly $20 million in annual revenue—an achievement he is justifiably proud of. But three business acquaintances started companies in the same industry at about the same time. The revenue of one company reached $300 million, the second exceeded $120 million, and the third grew to $75 million before they were sold. It is no surprise that all three sold for more than Dick's company. But none of those business owners worked as hard or as long as Dick, and they didn't have his academic credentials or his business experience. So how could they build companies that were so much more valuable than Dick's company? What did they do that he didn't?

The answer is they took action to increase the value of their company earlier than Dick. For example, all three had partners from day one, while

Dick built a management team only a few years before he sold the company. With partners, they were able to win new business with more clients, develop internal processes, and concentrate on their areas of strength. Dick, on the other hand, was spread too thin to do all the things required to grow his company.

They also made different hiring choices. They hired employees to build client relationships, while Dick was the main salesman and hired employees for their technical skills. They built partnerships with other companies, while Dick usually operated independently. In short, their companies were better connected and had a stronger management team, which made their companies more attractive to buyers.

To sell your company, a buyer must be convinced that your business is a solid investment with few risks. The first thing a buyer will want to see, of course, is the financial condition of the business. He'll want to see increasing sales and profits, and a cash flow that will support operating and financing costs starting the day the deal is closed. If buyers don't see a glowing financial future, they will either walk away or try to steal the business for a low price that pays them to fix what you didn't. Unfortunately, business owners get so involved in operations that they don't think about, plan for, or take action to improve their business. The information in this chapter will help identify where you might begin to make such improvements in your business.

While factors beyond anyone's control can derail a transaction, there are things you can do to maximize your chances for success. First, be objective in understanding why you want to sell, what you will do after the sale, and how much cash you will need for the lifestyle you want. Second, set your expectations by learning the M&A process and finding out how much your company is worth today. Third, recognize that you are emotionally involved in your business, and separate those emotions from a logical analysis of alternatives. Being clear about your objectives from the start will reduce later disappointment and aggravation during the lengthy sales process. Furthermore, there are several organizational, financial, and legal actions that will make your company more attractive to buyers and reduce the time and expense of the sale transaction.

If you aren't among the few business owners who begin to plan their exit from the start, planning to sell your business probably will begin the day you first realize you don't want to run it forever. Planning ends and execution begins when you entertain an offer from a potential buyer or you hire an investment banker (i.e., broker) to find a buyer. This chapter describes the actions to take before you begin a sale transaction, while Chapter 3 provides advice about negotiating and closing the deal as the seller. Effective planning two or more years before a sale can easily increase your after-tax proceeds by 20 percent or more. On a $5 million transaction, that's a million dollars more in your pocket!

During the planning phase, it is important to build a company that buyers will see as high value and low risk. In egregious cases, owners actually do things that make their exit difficult and reduce the value of their businesses. Entrepreneurs who excel in business do not succeed because of how much they know; they succeed because they recognize the need to change and make the change happen! Similarly, businesses don't fail because their owners lack operations, sales, or finance skills (they may, but such holes can be filled with a key hire); instead, they fail because they bury themselves in operations and complain about market conditions, competitors, and clients. Successful entrepreneurs are committed to succeed no matter what. Reading this book indicates you probably are one of those people—determined to succeed.

This chapter presents common mistakes that business owners make long before a transaction even begins. The mistakes are related to:

- Lack of clear objectives and a well-defined exit strategy
- Having clients and services/products that are not transferable
- Lack of a defined growth strategy
- A weak executive team
- Lack of written operating procedures
- Warts on the company's balance sheet or income statement
- Unrealistic expectations about the sale process

If you're serious about selling your company, you'll have a list of action items after you read this chapter. The list will seem daunting at first, but start with the easiest items first. If you are a buyer, this chapter will help you identify owners who are ready to sell their business versus owners who are trying to sell a business with weaknesses that you must fix.

MISTAKE #1

FUZZY OBJECTIVES

Think of your business as a way to achieve your objectives rather than an objective in itself, as an activity that enriches your life rather than an obligation that consumes your energy.

For personal reasons, a business owner's urgent objective was to sell his professional practice in order to move to a new state and then build a new practice there. Those sound like pretty clear objectives, don't they? But he got so focused on the need to relocate that he didn't consider the buyer's needs and characteristics, the transferability of the practice to a new owner, or his personal financial situation and future requirements.

The seller realized that his practice had little value without a facility because of the business' special zoning restrictions. The seller had been leasing his current facility, but that lease wasn't transferable. Therefore, the seller decided it would make financial sense to buy another practice that owned its facility, build the practice for a year so, and then sell the combined practice and facility. But the seller was reluctant to take on a larger practice and financial obligation without a buyer locked in for the combined practice. These requirements caused the owner to try to focus on two very different and complex transactions at the same time.

An interested buyer was located quickly for the original transaction. However, because of the much larger sale price for the two-practice deal, the buyer could only proceed if the seller provided financing. The seller was willing to provide long-term financing if he was confident that the buyer would generate sufficient cash flow from the business to repay the loan.

The number of variables made it difficult to close the transaction because, until the seller finished acquiring the second practice, he could not determine the cash flow required to fund the acquisition or the cash flow available to the buyer and him. Only then could the seller set a sale price and determine the amount of seller financing that he must provide. The buyer, on the other hand, was concerned that even the combined practice wouldn't provide sufficient cash flow to make loan payments to the seller and fund the lifestyle he wanted. The collision between the seller's need for cash to fund the new acquisition and the buyer's desire to grow the practice to deliver an acceptable income stream was an obstruction to finalizing a set of deal terms.

The seller proposed several different structures to keep the deal alive, such as making the buyer an employee and giving him the option to purchase the combined practice at the end of a year. The seller offered incentives to the buyer to exercise the purchase option but insisted on penalties if the buyer failed to exercise the option. To no one's surprise, the deal fell apart at that point. The lesson learned from this convoluted transaction is that being clear about your objectives and taking time to prepare your business for transfer to a buyer will increase the odds that your deal will close.

Closer to home, Dick thought he was clear about his objectives. By selling the company, he felt he would be financially secure and would have time to consult with CEOs and travel with his wife and family. He started preparing in earnest for an exit about two years before the event. Stuart helped him set up a family trust to manage and protect proceeds of the sale in a tax-advantaged way. But one thing Dick didn't anticipate in his plan was a near-50 percent plunge in the stock market a year after closing the sale. His financial planning assumed the stock market would continue to rise— with the usual downs and ups—like it always had. The price he had to pay for making that overly optimistic assumption was a cutback in his lifestyle. The market's big drop illustrates the importance of being conservative in your assumptions about the performance of financial markets and the rate of return on your investments.

Entrepreneurs usually acquire a company because they: (1) discover a lucrative opportunity, (2) want to be their own boss, or (3) can earn more money. Some start a company in bad times just to survive. Regardless of why you started yours, we recommend that the best time to begin planning your exit is when you start your company. Many new business owners ignore that advice, and don't give much thought to how or when they will exit their business. But as years pass, a variety of factors push them to think about leaving their company. The most common factors are:

- Retirement age approaches or health issues appear
- The owners want more leisure time
- A once-stimulating business becomes a drudgery
- The owners require increased liquidity
- Owners don't want to deal with the new economic environment
- Reluctance to transform operations to embrace new technologies
- Capital is needed to expand the business, but it isn't available
- Management is stretched too thin to cover expanding operations
- Conflict in the management team jeopardizes the business
- A management succession is not available from the executive team or within the owner's family

These factors have solutions besides leaving the company, of course, but owners who experience them may see selling as an instant cure. It's not! If you are having any of those feelings, resist jumping into a disruptive exit strategy until you are clear about your personal objectives, and have taken definitive steps to increase the value of your business.

Before starting to plan an exit strategy, it is helpful to answer a series of introspective questions. For example: Why did you begin or acquire the company in the first place? And have you achieved your original objectives? The other personal questions reside in four areas:

Post-Exit Lifestyle:

- By what date or event would you like to exit?
- Do you want to leave the business partially or completely?
- If you stay, would it be as a manager, a consultant, or a mentor?
- If you stay, will you be willing to work in a subservient role?
- What will you do in the next phase of your life?

Financial Requirements:

- How much money do you need and for what purposes?
- How will you manage and invest proceeds from the sale?
- Do you need all cash up-front, or can you finance the buyer?
- If you're willing to finance the deal, what will be your security?
- How much money, if any, will you pass to future generations?
- What are the income tax consequences of the sale?

Nature of the Buyer:

- Is it viable to transfer ownership to a family member?
- Is your preference to sell to your partners or key employee(s)?
- Are you willing to sell to a competitor, supplier, or customer?
- Would you sell to an outsider who only wants a financial interest?

Continuity of the Business:

- Do your partners know what you are thinking, and do they agree?
- How will your employees and family be affected by your exit?
- Will you or your employees insist on employment guarantees?
- How important is continuity of service to customers?

We suggest that you write your answers to these questions on paper and discuss them with your significant others and partners in the business. For now, don't worry about current market conditions or the readiness of your business to be sold. Those questions are less important than your personal objectives and are addressed later in this chapter.

Once you are clear about how you want things to be after your exit, and realize what it will take to give you the freedom and resources to be yourself, then you can develop an exit strategy and timetable that will fulfill your objectives. Such an exit strategy will give you peace of mind and allow you to return to the business with renewed dedication. Your written exit objectives are a clear statement of what selling the company must do for you. Thinking forward enables you to see your business as a means to achieve your objectives, a way to enrich your life rather than an obligation that consumes your time and energy.

MISTAKE #2

VAGUE EXIT STRATEGY

In order to leave on your terms with your desires met,
develop and implement a flexible exit strategy and timetable.

Two failed attempts to sell his business taught Dick that he needed a detailed exit strategy, rather than a vague notion that someday he would sell the business and sail happily into the sunset. In both cases, he would have been required to remain with the company after the sale. But Dick knew he didn't have the desire or personality to be an employee in his former company. In addition, he and his wife knew when they wanted to start retirement and how much they required from the sale so Dick no longer had to work. With professional help, he developed and executed a flexible exit strategy that he called *"Plan A, Plan B, & Plan C."*

Plan A, Dick's #1 preference, was to transfer company ownership to employees. He started a stock sale program where employees purchased stock through payroll deductions and bonuses. (Note: employees owned 35 percent of the stock when the company was sold.) He worked with the management team to create a brand that differentiated the company from competitors; and he involved them in developing strategies, setting goals, and designing procedures. The management team participated in Board of Directors meetings, one as a member and the others as regular presenters. Dick had experts determine the current value of the company and implement an algorithm to estimate how much it was worth at the end of each month. Unfortunately, when the time came to underwrite the loan to buy 100 percent ownership, the management team decided that they were unwilling to assume personal liability for the loan and did not proceed with the buyout.

Plan B, Dick's #2 preference, was structured to be put in place if the employees were unable or unwilling to buy the company. Plan B was to sell his ownership interest to a strategic buyer who could parlay the company's client base into rapid growth, or to a financial buyer who would use it as a platform for an IPO or roll-up. He was confident Plan B would work because he had been approached frequently by potential buyers and the company's contracts were for government services, a hot market after 9/11. He also attended seminars to learn what buyers were looking for, and hired consultants to help him maximize the company's value and eliminate things that might worry a potential buyer.

If Dick failed to find a third-party buyer who offered an acceptable price, he intended to implement Plan C: retire from daily operations and serve as Chairman of the Board. With the business organized as a Subchapter-S corporation, his income would be derived from current earnings. To prepare for Plan C, Dick began to work part time. First four days a week, then three days, and finally two days a week at the time the company was sold. He mentored the management team to set strategies, negotiate contracts, and make hiring decisions. He also implemented strict cash management procedures to ensure there would be sufficient cash to support his retirement. But psychologically, Dick knew that Plan C would be challenging because it would require him to surrender control to the management team and accept their operating decisions.

Actually, Dick's preparations for Plan A, Plan B, and Plan C were good for the company in general. For example, building a management team strong enough to buy the company was essential for Plan A, *and* it increased the company's value in the eyes of the eventual third-party buyer (Plan B) and allowed Dick to begin to remove himself from daily operations (Plan C). Likewise, the cash management process so vital in Plan C produced a clean balance sheet that supported bank financing for a management buyout (Plan A) and yielded cash flows that were very attractive to third-party buyers (Plan B).

Something like an A-B-C strategy would be useful for your exit too. One way or another, someday you will leave your company—willingly or unwillingly, alive or dead. Once you take the plunge and become a business owner, there are just six exit options:

(1) Transfer ownership to a family member(s)

(2) Sell the company to an employee(s)

(3) Sell the company to an outsider

(4) Become an absentee owner

(5) Liquidate the company (i.e., sell assets individually)

(6) Run the company until you die

You may choose any option(s) you like, and each option has multiple variants. But if you fail to make a conscious choice, by default you will be choosing exit option (6). If you choose several alternatives like Dick did, you can order them as first choice, second choice, etc. It turns out that things you do to prepare for your top alternative will also help most of the other options. The important thing is to begin planning your exit strategy and timetable long before your target exit date.

A key question in your exit planning is: *Are you willing to continue as an employee or consultant after you sell the business*? It's axiomatic in the M&A community that most entrepreneurs become unemployable after they have been their own boss for a few years. If you exit partially, are you ready to work for someone else? How will you react when they ignore your advice and/or run the business in ways that you don't like? If your answer is *NO*, what will you do after you sell the business?

In developing the timetable for your exit, ask yourself if getting the highest price for your business is most important, or is exiting as soon as possible the most important? Unless your company is in near-perfect shape with respect to sales, marketing, profitability, and staffing, if you want to exit quickly, you will probably need to discount the asking price and hope the buyer will be willing to fix the things that you haven't. If your priority (or need) is the highest possible price, allow two years or more to make the business highly attractive to multiple potential buyers.

Lastly, for several reasons, it is essential that you determine the value of your company today. First and foremost, today's value will determine if a sale would produce enough cash for retirement, to liquidate debts, to finance future entrepreneurial activities (if you are planning any), and to support the lifestyle you would like. The value of your business also will determine the type and magnitude of tax issues related to the sale. It is vital that you be able to say to yourself: *"I can sell when the company is worth more than $X."* Then it is up to you to take the actions required to make it worth that much (or more) using the techniques described in the remaining parts of this chapter.

MISTAKE #3

ARTIFICIAL DEADLINES

Your M&A transaction won't close when you would like it to—it will close when the market delivers a buyer who is willing to pay a price that you are willing to accept.

In 2006, near the peak in the M&A market, the owner of a chain of retail stores obtained a formal valuation of his holdings. He wanted to know how much his stores were worth because he and his wife had set his sixtieth birthday—which was only three years away—as the target date for their retirement. As the retirement date approached, his wife pushed him into action by repetitively asking, "*When will we retire?*"

His same-store sales increased 12 percent in 2007, but were flat in 2008. Early in 2009, he put the stores on the market expecting to receive roughly the 2006 valuation. His broker offered only bad news, saying that market values had dropped substantially, to which the owner said: "*I'll get my price even today!*"

After conducting a limited auction, the best offer was 25 percent lower than the 2006 valuation. It's not unusual for the gap between the buyer's offer and seller's expectations to be near 10 percent—a gap that's fairly easy to fill during negotiations. But a 25 percent gap is challenging. The seller provided a copy of the 2006 valuation to the buyer, who countered by offering payments under a consulting and not-to-compete contract, and an earn-out based on sales growth.

Then issues arose with financing. The buyer's bank said two years ago they granted loans where principal and interest payments were 110 to 125 percent of a business' disposable cash flow. In the 2009 market, the bank wanted cash flow to be 125 to 150 percent of principal and interest. Furthermore, the seller's accounting records were a mess, making it difficult to calculate cash flow accurately. For example, the seller had used company funds to buy benefits for himself, numbers that needed to be backed out to get a true estimate of actual profits. According to the Letter of Intent (LOI), the sixty-day due diligence window began when the seller provided financial data that met the bank's needs, so the transaction was delayed while the buyer performed an audit of 2007 and 2008. Despite these bumps, the parties hope to close the deal before the capital gains tax increase expected in 2011.

Hard deadlines for selling a business are a double-edged sword. You need a target date for planning purposes, but when the date is locked in concrete, it usually costs you money. Allowing personal factors such as retirement, family events, financial needs, or failing health to dictate the timing of the sale often reduces the price. Also, selling to take advantage of favorable tax provisions can reduce the price and make transactions more difficult. For example, banks rarely respond well to deadlines. So if you must choose between selling when you are ready or selling when the market is ready, clearly it's advantageous to sell when the market is ready. That being said, you never know when a buyer with deep pockets will knock on your door. That's why it is very important to complete the internal preparations discussed in this chapter: get annual audits, remove financial warts, brand your company, document procedures, build your management team, accurately predict sales and profits, and so on.

If you are planning to sell your company in the near future, you may be wondering how external factors like an economic boom or bust will affect your chance of finding a buyer. The good news is that if you have a profitable, growing company, you will always find a buyer. However, getting top price is a different matter. While unemployment is high and the real estate market is depressed, there may actually be buyers looking for a company like yours who normally wouldn't be looking during boom times. For example, some executives who get caught in layoffs at big companies will go into business for themselves—and buying your business may be a quick way to get started. Nobody says that selling a business is easy under any circumstances. But if you have a company with a rosy future, there are plenty of buyers who will be interested.

Getting top dollar for your company is a matter of timing. Markets change rapidly, so your business must be ready to sell when the market is hot in your industry. In addition to internal factors under your control, four external factors affect the price you are likely to receive:

- **General Economy:** When the general economy is booming, prices tend to peak because there are generally more buyers than sellers.
- **Your Industry:** Similarly, hot industries attract new investors, and businesses in such industries command higher prices.
- **Your Geographic Region:** Even in these tough times, for example, the south is growing and attracting new capital and employees.
- **Financing:** When financing is tight, buyers have difficulty raising cash to make deals, which depresses prices in most cases.

So the "perfect storm" that produces dream prices happens when the overall economy is booming, your industry is hot, you are located in a growing region, and financing is easy. Those conditions existed recently, and we will probably see them again in the future.

Major tax changes also affect the ideal timing of a sale. For example, economists expect that the capital gains tax will increase to 20 percent or more (it's 15 percent as of this writing) on January 1, 2011. That means business owners will keep 5 percent more of the proceeds if they sell before December 31, 2010. It's likely that bankers and M&A professionals (e.g., brokers, CPAs, and lawyers) will be busy near the end of 2010—so build your team now! It is also likely that an increase in the number of businesses for sale will create a buyer's market and reduce sales multiples.

Transactions that must close by a fixed date (e.g., by December 31st) rush banks to underwrite acquisition loans. Therefore, if a fixed closing date is required for your deal, the purchase contract should specify that a commitment letter must be received no later than 60 days before closing to allow the bank to complete its due diligence for the loan.

You can't control financial markets, of course, but you can be ready internally for the next "perfect storm." In terms of price, the ideal time to sell is when buyers see a peak in future earnings with no investment in new plants, equipment, or employees. Buyers sometimes walk away when they see a sales peak in the past, or the need to invest to produce growth. In any case, all M&A deals share a common attribute: The deal won't close when you want it to; it will close when the market provides a buyer that is willing to pay a price you are willing to accept!

MISTAKE #4

GETTING SOFT ADVICE— OR NONE AT ALL

Effective business advisors may cause you to feel uncomfortable as they push you to achieve higher goals and encourage you to fix things that aren't working.

Quarterly Board of Directors meetings at Dick's company felt like a root canal at a dentist's office. The Board had seven members: the President, Dick, and five business leaders whose only link to Dick was their roles as directors. The Board members' probing questions forced the executive team to prepare diligently for Board meetings, to develop viable plans-of-action to solve performance issues, and to provide facts and figures to validate market assumptions and revenue projections.

This governance process was highly valuable because it forced Dick and the executive team to openly and honestly examine quarterly results, projections for the future, and investment strategies—nothing soft about this Board's advice. Their thorough analyses pushed the executive team to make hard and often uncomfortable choices. Far from resenting those painful discussions, Dick respected the Board's guidance in growing the company and increasing its market value. He was grateful that the Board told him when he was doing something stupid—before he did it!

Jack Welch, legendary former CEO of General Electric, said: *"Too many executives avoid making hard decisions and thereby hurt not only their company but, in the long run, themselves."* One way to ensure you are making the hard choices is to surround yourself with advisors who provide cogent advice and hold you accountable to produce results. Four consistent sources of such advice are a: (1) Board of Directors (BOD) or Board of Advisors (BOA), (2) CEO peer group, (3) CPA or attorney, or (4) business consultants.

Dick required a BOD whose decisions were binding on the company because most employees owned stock and he had to ensure the company operated in a manner that benefited all shareholders. Board members were elected based on industry-specific experience in financial management, business development, strategic partnerships, operations, and M&A transactions. When majority interests are owned by a few owners, conflicts of interest may arise around decisions that directly benefit the majority owners versus other shareholders. In such cases, an independent Board of Directors can resolve the concerns of minority shareholders relative to conflicts of interest.

On the other hand, some closely-held companies establish a Board of Advisors (BOA) that makes recommendations, not binding decisions. BOA members often are selected by the owner rather than being elected by shareholders. Directors have legal and fiduciary responsibilities to the shareholders, but advisors don't. Therefore, it is easier to attract business leaders to serve on a BOA than on a BOD. Since a BOA provides guidance to grow a company but rarely delves into operations, BOA members have different qualifications than BOD members, but the owners must be willing to accept their recommendations. If you, as an owner, can listen to a BOA and take action on their advice without letting your ego interfere, then you could be well served with a BOA. However, if you cannot or will not accept and implement their recommendations, then you should have a BOD or nothing at all. To quote Clint Eastwood: *"A man must know his limitations."*

CEO peer groups like VISTAGE or CEO-Project also are sources of frank business advice. Dick recalls his CEO group meetings as candid discussions of core issues. If a CEO presented an issue but omitted facts or minimized his contributions to the problem, another CEO would call him on it. He says that at his very first CEO meeting, an issue was being discussed, and the presenter resisted the group's advice. A second CEO halted the dialog and said: *"Wait a minute. You don't have to do what we recommend, but you do have to listen."* Those are the kind of blunt advisors you want around to help grow your revenue and profits!

Are you getting the blunt legal and financial advice needed to operate a successful business and prepare it to be sold? Your attorney and CPA should be willing to tell you like it is—to explain the risks, the pitfalls, and the alternatives surrounding the strategic decisions you face. If you have an advisor who is more concerned about keeping you as a client than telling you when you're wrong, fire that advisor!

Small companies usually don't need, nor can they afford, a full-time lawyer. To operate on sound legal basis, however, they need a lawyer to help prepare standard contracts for use with shareholders, employees, customers, and consultants and to review contracts for joint ventures, leases, intellectual property rights, and so on. For example, a buy-sell agreement protects the value of a company by avoiding litigation among owners and preventing a minority shareholder from obstructing the sale.

Similarly, when Dick's company could only afford a controller, he received financial advice from a CPA who served as a "virtual CFO." The virtual CFO visited the company twice a month to review financial performance, evaluate financial processes and controls, and participate in the financial side of strategic planning events. He also participated in quarterly BOD meetings when financial topics were on the agenda.

Business owners who are determined to learn and grow often retain consultants to assist in areas like:

- Business development processes and tools
- Public relations and branding the company
- Organizational roles and responsibilities
- Documenting operating procedures
- Employee training programs
- Recruiting processes and hiring practices
- Incentive programs for executives and employees
- Annual operating plans, staffing projections, and budgets

Entrepreneurs rarely succeed because of what they know; more often they succeed because they can find the right answers. They instinctively know which areas are critical, where to get answers quickly, and how to improve business processes and hold employees accountable for results.

If you feel uncomfortable with what your Board, CPA, attorney, or consultants are suggesting, they are probably doing a good job. At the end of the day, of course, you choose to do or not do what they suggest after you have heard the alternatives and understand the consequences of your choices. Effective business advisors may push you in ways that feel uncomfortable—something that friends may be reluctant to do.

MISTAKE #5

NOTHING TO SELL

You might not have time to do everything you'd like to do, but finding time to build a sellable company is vital to your future.

An entrepreneur approached Dick during a networking breakfast and asked about how to sell his business. Eager to help a new client achieve his objectives, Dick agreed to meet the business owner in his office the next day. Overnight, Dick researched the web for information about the owner and the company. He found news stories and articles written by the entrepreneur, but there was no website for the company.

At the meeting, the business owner proudly explained how he had provided growth strategies, marketing plans, and branding tactics for mid-sized companies for more than twenty years. His track record was extraordinary, and he had a slew of customer success stories. His annual revenue was over $2 million, and he had five employees: three junior assistants who conducted workshops and prepared reports, an office manager, and a full-charge book-keeper. Dick listened and asked probing questions, but in the end, he had to tell the entrepreneur that, in the business' current form, he had nothing that anyone would buy. He had been so busy helping customers and supervising employees that he never built a business that was sellable.

We have met dozens of people like this entrepreneur. They are sales consultants, financial planners, website developers, technology wizards, and craftsmen. Most of them are highly educated professionals who are good at what they do and make a good living doing it. But they probably will work forever or retire based on IRA contributions they siphon from current earnings. The business itself is the main source of income to the owner and his family, and the owner has no desire to formalize its operations. So, if your headquarters is your home, you provide services in a highly competitive market, your processes and financial records are in your head, and your customers are also good friends, then your business will be difficult to sell since it would only have value to an entrepreneur who is looking to replace you in your lifestyle business.

On the other hand, if you own valuable intellectual property, such as patents and trademarks, repeatable written procedures and reports, technical documents, training courses, and workshop curricula, then you have something to sell to a broad market. All too often business owners get caught up in the day-to-day challenges of winning and keeping customers, and when the time comes to exit, they have few options.

To be interesting to a new owner, the business must be capable of being operated without the original owner, and it must be transferable to the new owner. The essential transferable assets the buyer will look for include:

- A unique product or service that can be delivered or sold by a staff
- Customers who are loyal to company, not the previous owner
- Written contracts with customers, suppliers, and distributors
- Documented business processes and procedures
- Licenses for proprietary processes and software systems
- A predictable stream of revenue, profits, and cash flow
- A management team that can operate the business without you
- Employment agreements with key employees
- Insurance and other benefit programs
- An identifiable presence and favorable reputation in the market
- Desirable location(s)
- Long-term leases for property and equipment
- Professional-looking facilities and up-to-date equipment.

If you start with the intent to develop a business that has these features, then you will have something that can be transferred to your employees or family, or sold to an outside buyer.

As you develop and execute your business plan, consider how you will accumulate assets that are easily transferable and how the business will operate without you. At a minimum, you will be able to take a vacation and still earn money while you are enjoying yourself in an exotic place!

MISTAKE #6

NO PLAN TO MAXIMIZE VALUE

Once you've built a business that is sellable, your next challenge is to measurably increase its value.

A business owner had a sellable company in a stable industry, and a good financial plan for his exit. His plan was to move to Arizona where he wanted a million dollars to build and furnish a new house on a lot he already owned (net after selling his current house), $2 million to pay off business and personal debts, half a million dollars for a travel fund, and $15,000 each month (after tax) for everyday living expenses. His financial advisor recommended a $7.5 million annuity to provide the monthly income and said that, all together, proceeds from selling the business had to total $11 million. The business owner wanted to know what to do to make his company worth that much.

In his industry, price multiples were 0.6 to 0.8 times revenue and five to seven times EBITDA, which is a measure of pre-tax cash flow. From a buyer's perspective, more cash flow means a higher value. So his business had to generate $14 to $18 million in annual revenue and produce an EBITDA of $1.6 to $2.2 million depending on whether the buyer valued the company at the low or high end of the multiples range. He already had a plan to increase revenue and EBITDA. But how could he position his company to be at the high end of the multiples range?

We evaluated the company against the 17 factors (see Appendix) that determine value for buyers of similar-sized firms in his industry. It rated above-market in four factors and equal-to-market in ten. The three below-market factors were:

(1) *Management Team:* The senior managers lacked depth and didn't grasp the company's strategic priorities. Since he planned to leave the company after closing, a strong management team was vital.

(2) *Business Pipeline:* His business had a history of winning renewal contracts, but no reliable process to manage new opportunities and accurately predict contract signings and future revenue.

(3) *Budgeting:* The business had no annual budget, profits were low, and Days Sales Outstanding (DSO) were high because of erratic billing practices and receivables follow-up.

It took twenty months to develop and implement the action plan to improve these three areas, then he hired a broker to market the company. Six months later, he closed the sale for 0.83 times revenue and walked away with almost a million dollars more cash than his financial target, which was fortunate because the stock market tanked and his annuity return was lower than expected.

Looking at your business through the eyes of a buyer will pay huge dividends. How do its growth rate, pipeline, profits, and financial ratios compare to other companies in the same industry? What areas are weak relative to your competitors, and how can you neutralize or eliminate the weaknesses that you identify? What are your strong points, and how can you showcase them in your branding and go-to-market strategy? Buyers especially trust what they learn about your business *before* they meet with you and hear your obviously biased description of the company.

Since buyers evaluate future earnings potential based on prior years' earnings, you will usually get the highest price when your company is approaching a peak in its earnings curve. Your position on that curve is determined by both internal and external factors. The external factors are related to market conditions and the economy, which, in general, you cannot change.

On the other hand, you have full control over the investments you make for internal improvements that push your company toward peak revenue and profits. Most businesses reach a size plateau where they can only grow further by investing in more risky and expensive expansions. If you have a services business, you may need to diversify its offerings, penetrate new clients, or expand into new geographic markets. If your company produces products, you may need to open a new facility, buy additional equipment, hire more sales staff or employees, or invest in a new technology. It's ideal if you can time your sale to occur just before the approach of a revenue peak, and manage your growth strategy and process improvements toward achieving that peak.

In maximizing the value of your company, consider three different types of outside buyers:

- A ***strategic buyer*** is a company in a line of business similar to yours. Their objective in buying your company is to expand their customer base, capabilities, competitiveness, or offerings.
- A ***financial buyer***'s goal is to earn a fair return on the investment, liquidate the acquisition loan from cash flow, and build equity for a future sale—all while someone else runs day-to-day operations.
- A ***lifestyle buyer*** is looking to buy your company because it will provide a rewarding work experience and deliver an acceptable salary and benefits to the new owner.

Each of the three buyers has a different way of determining how much they will pay for your business, but the actions you take to maximize your company's value will be viewed positively by all of them.

Failing to take timely action to increase the value of your company can be an expensive oversight. We often see business owners stuck in the quicksand of day-to-day operations. They forget that the company is their most valuable asset, and when a buyer comes along, they are left with *I-meant-to-do-it* fixes that reduce the selling price. Few business owners realize that it takes about two years to prepare a company to be sold for a top multiple. When M&A markets are in a dormant state, it is an ideal time to begin shaping your business to maximize its value and be ready for the boom market when it returns.

MISTAKE #7

ORGANIZATIONAL A-D-D

As the business owner, your job is to build an efficient and effective team—then get out of their way!

The workshop speaker opened his presentation to a group of business owners with an explicit challenge: *"If a bomb exploded right here, right now, who would replace you as the leader of your company, and would they succeed?"* Most admitted they had no clear successor, and the few who had designated one expressed substantial concerns about his or her ability to manage and grow the company. Even though Dick's company was over fifteen years old at the time, he was in the majority that didn't know who their successor would be. His company probably would have disintegrated if he had been hit by the proverbial bus.

It was a jolting wake-up call. Like many business owners, Dick was involved in every aspect of the company's operations from accounting to project management to business development. He fantasized about the cash he would get when he sold the company, but he had done little to build an organization that was capable of succeeding without him. When he returned to his office that afternoon, he e-mailed the top people in the company and asked: *"If I got hit by a bus on the way home today, what part of our operations would be your biggest problem tomorrow?"* Their responses were unexpectedly passionate and varied.

The issues were compiled in a written plan. In addition to expected concerns about Dick's relationships with Board members, bankers, key customers, and strategic partners, they were worried about:

- Lack of written procedures for project and financial management
- Personnel policies that were outdated and often not followed
- The ad hoc nature of decisions about pricing, hiring, and salaries
- Erratic business development priorities and actions

In short, Dick's company suffered from a severe case of organizational *Attention*

Deficit Disorder (A-D-D): Employees jumped from one of his priorities to the next without knowing why or being given consistent guidance. He frequently blamed others for not reaching annual revenue and profit goals, but organizational A-D-D was the real cause. He had been doing everyone's job except for his own, which was to point the company toward its goals, get out of the way, and let his highly capable managers and employees do their jobs.

After a year of intense effort to address his managers' concerns and implement changes, Dick was surprised that the company's growth rate and profits both increased. The managers expanded client relationships and made more effective project management and financial decisions. In addition, Dick was able to reduce his working schedule to four days per week in the first year, and to three days per week after the second year. Employees joked that the company operated better than when Dick was working full-time! That may or may not have been true, but clearly the company was stronger because it had written procedures and managers had freedom and authority to operate the business. Because the company could run without Dick, it commanded a higher multiple in a sale.

It may seem paradoxical, but your company would be more valuable if it could operate without you. Any one individual, even someone as plugged-in and skilled as an effective CEO, can exercise a limited span-of-control and cultivate just a few relationships. If you feel you must be involved in every decision, you're the governor that limits the speed of growth because there aren't sufficient hours in a day for you to make every decision. Sustained growth requires business owners to transfer management responsibilities to their staff in order to free themselves to explore new markets, to win new clients, and to increase the company's market value.

Furthermore, if you feel compelled to make every decision, then your management team will be reluctant to make decisions without you. Your most effective managers may become frustrated by their lack of control and leave the company. In summary, your ability to retain the top talent required to increase the value of your company is significantly reduced by your over-involvement in decision-making.

Dick claims that he was the best business developer, proposal writer, project manager, and financial manager in his company. Unfortunately, as long as that statement was true, his company was unsellable. He was, in effect, the whole company, and the only thing a buyer would've been buying is Dick—yet he wanted to leave the company after the sale! After years of trying to be the best at everything, Dick finally built the staff's capabilities, established performance metrics, and backed away from daily operations. That made the company attractive to the equity investors who eventually purchased it, and allowed him to walk away and have little interaction with the company after the sale.

If you founded and built your own company, you undoubtedly are the most visionary, experienced, and skilled person on your entire staff. But if your company depends on you for survival, it is not worth very much without you, and there is no way you can exit. Change your *no-one-can-do-it-as-good-as-I-can* attitude by training your management team to operate effectively and efficiently without you. Ask yourself the following questions:

- *Whose job am I doing today?*
- *Who should be doing those things?*
- *How can I stop doing them and give responsibility to them?*

Successful business owners ask themselves these questions regularly, and use the answers to change their behaviors and build their staff's capabilities.

Your power as the business owner is the ability to attract talented employees, and set purpose and direction for the organization. In today's rapidly evolving business world, it isn't your peoples' arms and legs that will produce success—it is their hearts and heads. Your employees need to be led more than they need to be managed. In our experience, lack of passion in otherwise healthy and successful businesses is caused by lack of clear goals. When urgent but unimportant things divert your staff's attention from strategically vital tasks, organizational A-D-D may be the cause. The cure is for you to refocus your team's purpose—then get out of their way!

MISTAKE #8

AD HOC OPERATIONS

To maximize the efficiency and value of your business, design it around repeatable procedures rather than superstars.

If you have traveled domestically or internationally, you've probably noticed that McDonald's hamburgers are the same everywhere. It is no accident. Senior managers at every franchise are required to participate in training at the corporate facility known as "Hamburger University." In addition, McDonald's has detailed written procedures for every facet of the operation. What's more, because of those procedures, McDonald's is legendary for the entry level skills of its employees—they are the largest employer of high school students in the world. The business model that Ray Kroc devised is acknowledged as his greatest business contribution. In order to sell franchises, he built a model that worked no matter who purchased them. Specifically, it worked without him because franchise operations were designed around procedures, not superstars.

Dick was struck by the McDonald's phenomena during a vacation in St. Maarten. When he returned, he asked himself: "*Making hamburgers with high school kids is one thing, but how can I adapt that model to a company that delivers consulting services using MBAs?*" The answer took several years to discover. The result was the Integrated Change Management (ICM) methodology that was documented with project management (PM) procedures in the company's ICM/PM Manual. The manual was used in project work, in consulting and project management training, and as the basis for the certifications required for promotions. The ICM/PM Manual also was valuable to prospective buyers because it gave them confidence that the business could operate efficiently and effectively without Dick.

If your company doesn't already have and use a procedures manual, start developing one today. The manual should describe how things are done so employees (and a future owner) conduct business in a reliable, efficient, and repeatable manner—even if you aren't there to supervise. Typically, the manual will address the following topics, in addition to processes and procedures that are essential and unique to your industry:

- Organizational roles and responsibilities
- Recurring management meetings
- Business development strategies and marketing methods
- Sales reporting, quotas, and commissions
- Bidding, estimating, and contract review/approval
- Project management processes and responsibilities
- Product development, quality control, and delivery
- Customer service and warranties
- Billing and accounts receivable, including discounts, credits, returns, refunds, and special orders
- Purchasing, including purchase order approvals
- Shipping and receiving
- Cash management
- Normal business hours and after-hour and holiday procedures
- Equipment operations and maintenance
- Computer operations and security
- E-mail and web usage and website postings

Since procedures change often, there must be a process for collecting changes and updating the manual. Consider an online Wikipedia-like environment for your procedures manual because it is easy to maintain and avoids cumbersome distribution of hard-copy manuals.

Personnel policies manuals are normally separate from procedures manual, although they may be combined. While personnel manuals are largely boilerplate disclosures related to employment practices, a failure to have an up-to-date personnel manual could subject your company to costly employment litigation.

You may think it is excessive for your company to divert significant resources to document operating procedures. But in addition to greatly enhancing the attractiveness of a business to buyers, written procedures are good business practice. They are valuable for increasing operational quality, for branding the company as reliable and consistent, for training employees, and for continuously improving performance. ISO-9000 certifications and

Capability Maturity Model Integration (CMMI) appraisals are widely recognized and highly respected in this regard. Furthermore, written procedures will reduce operational complexity and less-qualified employees can fill positions when duties, procedures, and performance metrics are specified in writing.

A thorough procedures manual allows your company to appear well managed and less risky to prospective buyers. If your company has unique techniques for delivering a service or product, be prepared to show the buyer procedures that describe how you do it. The procedures manual will be relatively short if your operations are straightforward and simple. However, if your operations are complex, the procedures manual is likely to be longer and require considerable thought and time to prepare. Either way, a procedures manual is a high-value investment that will streamline operations in the short term, and increase the value of your company in the long term.

When you prepare the offering memorandum to sell your company, be sure to mention that written operating procedures and employment policies will be available for the buyer to review during due diligence. Since the manual is part of the "secret sauce" for your success, it should not be shown to the buyer until the due diligence phase of the sale.

Many business owners feel that their success depends on building an amazingly competent staff, including managers with advanced degrees from prestigious universities. But that's a mistake! It's difficult to find such people, and when you do, they are expensive, hard to retain, and a pain in the neck to deal with. Instead, what your company needs to be successful is effective procedures and training—a business model like McDonald's that will produce consistent results virtually independent of the people you hire. Such procedures will resolve many of your current challenges by streamlining decision-making in your organization or by eliminating the need for decisions in the first place. Furthermore, such procedures increase your company's value in an M&A transaction because they are exactly what buyers want to minimize risk! So build your company around procedures rather than superstars.

MISTAKE #9

WEAK EXECUTIVE TEAM

No matter what your exit strategy, building a capable and self-sufficient executive team is essential.

L ack of an effective executive team wreaks havoc in operations and M&A transactions. An entrepreneur was a thought leader in health care technology, and his contacts helped the company grow rapidly. On the other hand, his Achilles heel was placing people in executive positions for which they weren't qualified. For example, he hired average project managers and promoted the best one to Chief Operating Officer (COO). Similarly, he rewarded his bookkeeper with the title of Chief Financial Officer (CFO) and refused to hire a Vice President of Sales because he wanted that function for himself. Unfortunately, the lack of an effective COO and CFO caused operating errors that cost him millions and sunk his opportunity to sell the company.

During the dot-com era, he wanted to take his technology company public, so he accepted mezzanine funding from foreign investors. After the crash, they backed out and tried to recover their investments. Under terms of the agreement, he instructed the bank to release escrow funds, but not having a qualified CFO to oversee and complete the transaction in all respects, he failed to get releases from the investors in exchange for the funds. The matter is still in litigation.

In addition, he had difficulty closing government contracts. Auditors found that his CFO had added fees to subcontracts (which was explicitly prohibited in the contract) and overbilled the government by several million dollars. He thought the company was highly profitable, but it had negative net worth after he repaid the government and restated his financial statements. The good news is he is on the path to recovery. He has hired an experienced COO, a top-notch accounting firm, and a sales director. He still needs a CFO, but at least he's receiving quality advice from a CPA. He has plans to try to sell the company again in two years but has lots of work to do to make it attractive to buyers. He paid dearly for the lack of a self-sufficient executive team to help lead the company and keep it out of trouble. Competent managers don't necessarily make effective corporate executives.

That unfortunate situation reminded Dick of the CEO of a company who had been his subcontractor a few years earlier. He phoned the CEO to discuss a new opportunity that was ideal for teaming. The startled receptionist who answered the call said, *"I'm sorry. George died three weeks ago."* Dick was shocked and saddened by the news. He and George had shared the challenge of growing privately-held companies and, at one point, had discussed the possibility of merging their two companies. Opportunity missed. A startling realization crossed Dick's mind. In every case where Dick's company worked with George's company, George was the decision-maker for preparing proposals, negotiating contracts, and submitting bids. No other executive in his company ever made an important decision.

Dick continued by asking the receptionist, *"Who manages your sales and proposals now?"* She answered, *"We're still sorting that out."* It seems George's four vice presidents actually were project managers, and he didn't have an executive succession plan. The vice presidents were given the executive titles to increase their prestige with customers on the contracts they managed. They didn't participate in executive-level tasks like analyzing financial statements, negotiating contracts, and setting strategic directions for the company; George made all of those decisions by himself. Sadly, George's company went bankrupt about six months after his death.

Consider your business as a three-legged stool that falls over if any one of the three legs is weak. The three legs are:

- Delivering products and services creatively and efficiently, usually the responsibility of a COO.
- Marketing the company effectively to sell products and services to customers, usually the responsibility of a sales executive.
- Managing accounting, human resources, contracts, and facilities in a disciplined fashion, usually the responsibility of a CFO.

When you started your company, you probably did all three unless you had a partner to share the load. Which of the three functions is your personal strength? Which function is your weakest? Your weakest function is likely the area where the company's value is low, and probably should be the first position for which you hire a key executive. Specific people should be designated to manage each of these functions, and they should know at least as much as you know about that area—though it would be ideal to hire an executive with more knowledge than you relative to techniques and tools related to those functions. Is there such a person?

No matter what your exit strategy, a strong executive team is vital to success. If you plan to leave after selling the company, it is essential that all three positions be filled with qualified professionals while you focus on ways to build the company's value. Performance incentives and stock ownership plans that act like golden handcuffs, and strong employment agreements that prevent employees from damaging the company if they leave, are appropriate for most senior executives. Even if you don't plan to exit for years, filling the three positions will accelerate your company's growth, increase its profit, and give you freedom—plus it is good management practice!

One way to test the effectiveness of the executives in your company is to take an extended vacation. Each time you leave, designate of one of them to be acting CEO—and don't call into the office or tell them where you will be. When you return to the office, any issue that your executive team couldn't resolve without you is an opportunity for you to train a successor and explain the criteria for making decisions.

If your exit strategy is to sell your company to a key executive or the management team, the same principles apply. Groom the key executive to be the CEO. When you exit and he becomes CEO, he'll leave a hole in his former position, and the company will need a new CFO, COO, or VP of Sales. So each of your senior executives should have their own plan to develop their successor.

As Jim Collins tells us in his book *Good to Great*, when you get the right people in the right seats, everything gets easier!

MISTAKE #10

WHO OWNS THIS PLACE?

Selling part ownership in your company to one or more of your key executives is a matter that should not be taken lightly or done without legal advice.

Dubious stock ownership records are a common due diligence issue. For example, one CEO promised two key executives: *"I'll give you shares when I sell the company."* His intentions were good. It seemed to be a generous way to motivate them to grow the company and prepare it to be sold. The sale had advanced through most of due diligence when the CEO revealed his verbal agreements. He had promised one executive a 10 percent ownership stake (he had none) and the other a 20 percent stake (he already owned 10 percent). His attorney and CPA applauded the CEO's integrity...and then explained the tax consequences of a last-minute ownership transfer: The sale proceeds were subject to ordinary income taxes instead of lower capital gain taxes. Had the stock transfer agreement been documented a year or more before the closing, the executives would have earned substantially more from the transaction.

Another business originally had three equal shareholders. One of the owners wanted to leave the company, so the other two bought his stock for $5 million and obtained a form-letter release-of-claims. Six months later they put the company on the market and received a LOI for $150 million. However, the publicly-traded buyer was afraid the situation had created two classes of stock—prohibited in S-corporations—and insisted that the third owner sign a new release to acknowledge the pending sale. The two owners were uncomfortable with contacting the former owner, and offered to indemnify the buyer against any claims from him. The departed owner got wind of the sale and claimed that the value of the company had been misrepresented. Even though the third owner probably would not have won a lawsuit, the two owners paid him an additional $5 million to obtain the second release.

In a third case, a CEO had sold stock to employees for over twenty years and redeemed the stock whenever an employee left the company. All stock transactions were governed by a stockholders' agreement that employees signed when they first purchased stock. Unfortunately, in the early days of the plan, the company made an error in a stock repurchase: It redeemed fewer shares than the departing employee owned. Ten years and several stock splits later, the company was sold, and the error was discovered in due diligence. For starters, since the shareholder hadn't participated in distributions for several years, the company owed him nearly $80,000 in prior-year distributions. Even worse, because of the error, stock was issued to the CEO that exceeded the number of shares permitted by the Articles of Incorporation—thus the invalid sale to the CEO had to be reversed. The owner thought that he owned 84 percent of the stock, when actually it was about 70 percent. At closing, his portion of the sale proceeds was much less than he expected.

One way to hire, retain, and motivate key executives is to have them participate directly in the growth and success of the company. There are several ways to offer such an attractive incentive plan including:

- A *bonus plan* whereby, upon sale of the company, a percentage of the net sales price is allocated into a bonus pool which is then paid to key executives according to a preset formula.
- A *phantom equity plan* whereby executives are awarded shares of "phantom equity" that participate in annual earnings and/or sale proceeds, but are not actually a legal ownership interest.
- An *equity option plan* whereby the executives earn vested options to buy equity at a specified price sometime in the future, with the vesting becoming immediate if the company is sold.
- An *equity sale plan* for selling shares of stock to key executives on a regular basis often through payroll deductions and bonuses.

There are many variations of these plans, and each plan has different income tax impacts on the company and executives. For example, the first three plans provide tax deductions for the company and ordinary income for executives upon a sale, while proceeds in the fourth plan are capital gains for the executive but do not create a tax deduction for the company. The first two plans are simple to implement, but weak with regard to handcuffing the executive;

while the other two plans are more complex to implement but are stronger retention mechanisms. Since the benefits and costs of each plan are different, consult with your CPA and attorney before implementing any incentive plan. Such plans often increase the value of a company because a buyer will value highly any actions taken to retain motivated key executives.

For many entrepreneurs, starting a company meant investing most of their savings, taking a pay cut, and using their home as collateral for the line-of-credit. Some people are reluctant to take such risks. They say they want to own a business, but they don't want to jeopardize their paycheck. It is understandable, of course, but it is the visible difference between a risk-taking entrepreneur and a cautious individual who is comfortable being somebody's employee. Entrepreneurs willingly take risks and put everything on the line to achieve success. Sometimes they fail and are forced to start all over again. Folklore says that Walt Disney went bankrupt seven times before he finally succeeded.

You can recognize the entrepreneurs on your staff. They are the risk-takers, the ones who eagerly accept incentive compensation agreements as opposed to those who feel a sense of entitlement. Businesses large and small need entrepreneurs to grow rapidly and develop new products and services. High-growth companies often have several executives that are growth-oriented entrepreneurs in their hearts.

The most common exit strategy for a company founder is a buyout by an executive or family member. Such exits are convenient, but rarely problem-free. Most buyouts are successful once the initial hurdles are overcome. Statistics show that a typical leveraged buyout will double the value of the company in about four years. According to Dealogic, a New York research firm, leveraged buyouts on average begin with a debt-to-equity ratio of 85 percent, and deliver a return of 78 percent. While some of the high return is attributable to tax savings due to debt, the largest part of the gain comes from operational improvements implemented by the executive team after they complete the buyout.

Selling to employees through an Employee Stock Ownership Plan (ESOP) can produce income tax benefits for both seller and employee buyers. However, ESOP transactions are more costly to close and have significant annual administrative costs. An ESOP should be implemented only with support from experienced ESOP advisors.

In addition to financing challenges caused by lack of entrepreneurial savvy, conflicts in management styles are a chronic issue when giving ownership to a key executive. Let's assume that you plan to sell stock in your company to an executive who has expressed a desire to take over the company and demonstrated management expertise. He also must be a person who you trust and are willing to invest in, because most of the time you will finance his purchase. But when you sell him the first share of stock, he becomes your partner. For the partnership to thrive, the owners must cooperation and share mutual respect.

The most common way to begin selling ownership is to give a key executive stock in lieu of salary or bonus. Consult your attorney or CPA about income tax consequences for the executive and the company since they vary widely depending on the structure of the stock transfer. If an executive is unwilling to accept stock in place of cash compensation, then he may not possess the entrepreneurial spirit necessary to run the company, and you should reconsider your offer. Furthermore, there is no quicker way to create conflicts and jeopardize the value of the company than to implement this type of plan without the knowledge and consent of other key members of the management team. Selling stock in your company to one or more of your key executives is a matter that should not be taken lightly or done without legal advice.

Stuart tells his clients that having a partner is like being married without the sex. When things go bad, the only thing you have to fight over is money. To avoid expensive legal battles, insist on a strong buy-sell agreement before the first share of stock is transferred. The buy-sell agreement should specify what will happen if an executive shareholder dies, quits, or is fired; how serious management disagreements will be resolved; and what will happen if you, as the majority owner, decide instead to sell your ownership interests to someone else. We recommend that entrepreneurial spirit be a criterion in your decisions to hire or promote someone into an executive position in your company.

MISTAKE #11

FINANCIAL WARTS

*Look at your financial statements as if you were the
buyer—then take action to remove the ugly warts.*

A health care technology company who sold software-as-a-service (SAAS) was approached by a publicly-traded buyer. They negotiated a Letter of Intent (LOI) that included a clause whereby the seller certified itself to be debt-free. That provision was critical to the buyer because it was a condition of his source of funding for the transaction. The seller signed the LOI, confident that his balance sheet showed no debt.

Two damaging warts were discovered during due diligence because the seller had convinced his CPA to handle transactions off the balance sheet. The first transaction was the sale and lease-back of the seller's building, which was treated in balance sheet notes as if it were an operating lease. The buyer's CPA, however, saw it as a capital lease that should have been treated as an asset with offsetting debt. Furthermore, capital leases were specifically prohibited under the buyer's source-of-funding agreement. In the second transaction, the seller had licensed key production software using a five-year lease-to-purchase agreement, and treated the monthly payments as ordinary expenses. The buyer's CPA felt that they should be handled as a purchase with a long-term debt.

The accounting issues surrounding these two items, which seem like technicalities, delayed the transaction for almost a year. The good news is the transaction eventually closed, but not until a compromised price (several million dollars below the initial offer) was negotiated among the parties, including the buyer's source of funds. Lesson learned: Don't cajole your CPA into hiding transactions, because they will surely be discovered during due diligence, usually with expensive consequences.

The financial warts in this story were obscure. We see more obvious warts in almost every transaction. The list below provides a sampling of financial warts that are fairly common. Do you have any of them?

Balance Sheet:	- Sloppy cash management (unreconciled balances)
	- Uncollectible receivables or excessive write-offs
	- Overdue or unrecognized accounts payable
	- Non-transferable licenses
	- Lack of clear title to key production assets
	- Company assets primarily used by the owners
	- Personal property owned by the company
	- Poorly documented loans to or from the owners
	- Unprotected intellectual property
Unrecognized Liabilities:	- Undocumented ownership agreements
	- Expiring, non-transferable, or problematic leases
	- Pending lawsuits and contract disputes
	- Guaranteed retirement or health care for retirees
	- Underfunded retirement plan liabilities
	- Unfunded warranties or service agreements
Income Statement:	- Lack of a budget and spending controls
	- Dependency on a few clients for revenue
	- Contracts that are losing money
	- Understated cost-to-complete on fixed price jobs
	- Low operating margins and low net earnings

There's only one way to say it: *Ugly financial warts look even uglier to a buyer!* In addition to price implications, they undercut the buyer's confidence in the seller's management ability and honesty. Each of these warts (and others that aren't listed) will reduce the value of a company.

Removing warts is a good thing for your company even if you don't plan to sell in the near future. For example, it will improve your chances of getting a bank loan. Examine your financial statements, discuss them with your CPA, and ask: "*What items can be eliminated, and what items that should be there aren't?*" The findings will fall into two categories: personal items and business-related items.

Business owners, especially those who founded their companies, are notorious for co-mingling personal and business transactions. To groom the company to be sold, separate the two. Privately-held companies are operated to maximize after-tax income for the owners, so salaries and benefits may be manipulated to benefit the owner without regard to the bottom line. Assets the owners use that might be seen as liabilities by a buyer (e.g., golf club memberships, luxury cars, or a company airplane) should be transferred to the owners and removed from the balance sheet. If you want to retain such benefits, own them personally or through a separate business entity and lease them to your company at market rates with a cancellation clause that can be executed prior to closing a sale.

In addition, business owners often treat perks (e.g., conferences and travel) as compensation—their reward for working long hours with no extra salary. Such expenses should be minimized in the months before the company is offered for sale, although they can easily be added back to the bottom line in the offering statement.

For business items, get help from a CPA to restate your balance sheet by removing non-essential assets and assets you do not intend to include in the sale, and by reviewing the treatment of all liabilities. For example, the company may have idle cash in a money market account; there's no profit in selling cash. Instead, distribute the cash to owners as bonuses taxed as ordinary income, or dividends currently taxed as capital gains. If the company owns its building, you may want to transfer ownership to a separate entity that you own and lease it to your business. The buyer will have the option of purchasing the building or continuing to lease it depending on his ability to service additional debt. Consider treating vacant land and fully depreciated equipment the same way.

In general, try to remove loans from the balance sheet before offering the company for sale, especially those due-from or due-to the owners. Buyers usually won't assume short-term debt, so pay off revolving loans and lines-of-credit if possible. Taking these actions before due diligence will result in a clean and expeditious sale.

For companies with annual gross revenue in excess of $2 million, we recommend investing in an annual audit because private equity investors and large buyers often insist on at least two years of audited statements. Such audits can be done just prior to the sale, of course, but they will be more expensive, delay closing, and potentially uncover warts that can sink the deal. That's a great reason for having an annual audit this year and getting wart-removal advice from your CPA.

MISTAKE #12

HOCKEY STICK PROJECTIONS

If your projections of future revenue, profits, and cash flow seem too good to be true, buyers generally won't believe them and may walk away from the transaction.

An owner provided data for the revenue and profit projections in the offering memorandum. His sales during the previous ten years had been a sawtooth curve with more ups than downs with a compounded annual growth rate (CAGR) of 3 percent. Sales the preceding two years had been down 4 percent and up 16 percent, respectively, over the previous years, but he fearlessly projected 15 percent growth for each of the next five years. The sales graph literally looked like a hockey stick with the five future years being the long handle of the stick.

In the offering memorandum, he substantiated the sales projections by citing quotes from industry experts who predicted favorable market trends for his industry based on new technologies. He also included a table of quarterly forecasts from each of his salesmen justifying revenue projections for the coming year. The sales staff forecasted sales for a rolling four quarters.

Historically, the profit graph was erratic: two annual losses and three high-profit years in the last five. Profits in the preceding two years were a 5 percent loss and a 13 percent profit, respectively. Yet he projected a flat 10 percent profit each year for the next five years. To explain the unprofitable years, he said the company had been late in reducing staff and expenses after market downturns. The offering memorandum didn't contain cash flow projections.

When an interested buyer asked to see the salesmen's projections as of January 1st for the previous two years, only two salesmen could find them, and in both cases, actual sales for the year were measurably below the January forecasts for the year. No one was surprised when the buyer walked from the transaction. Eventually, the company was sold but at a multiplier well below industry average.

Projections have a large effect on the multiple and the selling price. Buyers purchase the future, so it's understandable that they expect to see reliable projections of revenue, profit, and cash flow. In addition, they want to understand the basis for the projections and the dependability of the methodology used to prepare them. Repetitious year-on-year growth projections are suspect because the real world doesn't operate that way.

Several years before Dick offered his company for sale, his Board of Directors challenged the sales and profit projections he presented at the January Board meeting—and the Board rejected the budget, hiring, and investment plans based on those projections. Board members helped Dick's company implement accurate projection techniques that included bottom-up sales forecasts and a bonus program for the sales staff based on both the dollar value of closed deals and the accuracy of their individual sales projections.

Since services under the company's contracts were delivered over many months, the controller developed an algorithm to convert sales projections into month-by-month revenue projections for a three-year period. Knowing the payment pattern for each customer also enabled the controller to project monthly cash flow. All of those projections were documented in the Annual Operating Plan (AOP) that included month-by-month staffing requirements, estimates of direct and overhead costs, end-of-month cash balances, and both the depreciation costs and cash flow impacts of new investments.

The accuracy of the first year's AOP projections was shaky—outside the plus-or-minus 10 percent range set by the Board. Each month, the management team reviewed actual results versus sale-by-sale and contract-by-contract projections to determine where and why last month's projections were incorrect. One by one, the root causes of inaccuracies were eliminated. When Dick offered the company for sale, three years of annual projections made in January were available for the buyer to compare to actual year-end sales and revenue for the same year. The AOP projections had high credibility with buyers, and were helpful in negotiating a line-of-credit with the bank. Dick now helps other companies implement this methodology, which is best practice in addition to increasing the value of a company.

We recommend you implement a method that enables you to show sales and profit projections at the beginning of a year and actual results at year's end. That will validate your forecasting technique and increase the buyer's confidence in your sales and budget projections even if they do look like a hockey stick! Two years of accurate (within 10 percent) projections are generally sufficient to establish credibility with a buyer. Most buyers tend to believe that if projections look too good to be true, then they probably aren't. Therefore, your revenue and profit projections should be reasonable, maybe even a little conservative.

Of course, the accuracy of your revenue and profit numbers depends on the accuracy of your sales projections. So the indispensable first step is implementing a disciplined methodology to select opportunities, track them through the sales process, and measure results. Dick admits that at one time in his company there was little rhyme or reason for opportunities his company pursued. But that all changed when the Board insisted that he implement an automated sales tracking system to manage the sales process. The sales managers were pushed to identify opportunities and report status in a standard way. Their results were routinely compared to their sales forecasts, which improved the overall sales process and the accuracy of their projections.

Since your #1 job as a business owner is to build and train your team, let your people wrestle with the challenges of projecting annual revenue and profits. By requiring his management team to present the new AOP to the Board in January and report quarterly results against the AOP at the April, July, and October Board meetings, Dick increased the value of the company, and was able to walk away after the sale closed. Likewise, you can build your management team's projection skills by removing yourself from the day-to-day action (other than as an advisor) and letting them prepare the strategic plan, make their projections, and own their results. Then, in addition to confidence in your projections, a prospective buyer will have confidence in the team's understanding of the market because of its ability to accurately forecast sales, revenue, and profits—then meet those forecasts.

MISTAKE #13

MILE WIDE AND AN INCH DEEP

Align your customer base and service/product offerings toward growth areas that will attract buyers. Eliminate the oddballs.

Most business owners work 24-7-365 to grow their companies. But even when their companies become substantial, they continue to operate in survival mode by chasing business from any customer who will pay them. Their goal is to grow big, and a large customer base looks like an easy way to get there. But in the long run, uncontrolled diversification is the glittering fool's gold of growing a business. Extreme diversification can become a growth-limiting addiction that stretches resources beyond the point of breaking. To grow in ways that add value to your company, escape the trap of thinking and acting like a small business even though it is difficult, risky, and uncomfortable.

Dick knows because he had to do it. His company started in 1984 with two subcontracts on Navy projects. The problem was that both subcontracts covered just his personal services. So during the first two years, the company had no other employees. His challenge was to stop selling himself and start building a real company that eventually he could sell. There is a simple and repeatable process for that. First, he became a valued advisor by helping customers plan their projects, justify their budgets, and produce results. Customers routinely asked for his analysis and recommendations prior to making major decisions.

Soon he was stretched in three ways: (1) he didn't have time to do everything his customers wanted; (2) they needed specialized expertise that he didn't have; and (3) simple tasks had to be done for which his hourly rate was excessive. Each of those situations was an opportunity to hire a new employee. Over the next several years, he converted the relationships into multi-year, small business set-aside contracts. Having built critical mass and developed a favorable reputation with customers, the company expanded by competing for contracts with other federal agencies.

The company was growing steadily, and the staff wanted to expand into higher profit, commercial work. Dick thought it was a good idea, so they marketed their IT expertise and won contracts with non-profits, a bank, a manufacturer, and several state and local government agencies. Dick later called this marketing strategy the "whack-a-mole" approach—his company went after any opportunity that popped up its head! At one point, the company had $7 million in annual revenue from contracts with eleven federal customers and nine other clients—an average of about $350,000 per client in a market where million-dollar contracts are common. His company's customer base was a mile wide but just an inch deep!

Then the roof fell in. A shift in the Navy's IT contracting strategy caused several of the company's bread-and-butter contracts to end. At the same time, the cost of marketing and servicing a scattered customer base was rising out of control. Dick's company had its first-ever annual loss even though everyone was working long hours.

Dick's initial survival action was to jettison low-margin customers and focus on federal business. One by one, the contracts with state and local governments, non-profits, and commercial firms ended. It hurt to watch customer relationships atrophy and to decline new opportunities in those sectors. But it was necessary to survive and increase the value of the company in eyes of buyers who would either want federal contracts or commercial contracts, but not a mixture.

In addition, as annual revenue neared the federal ceiling for a small business, Dick knew it was crucial to end the dependence on set-aside contracts. The company's value was a multiple of revenue, but buyers devalue set-aside contracts or won't consider buying a company whose portfolio includes set-aside contracts. So Dick weaned himself and his management team away from the small business contracting strategy.

They systematically converted the largest client relationships (which were all set-aside contracts) to multi-year, full-and-open contracts. The company's marketing efforts were directed toward agencies that require security clearances. Over a three-year period, the company won seven of eight full-and-open competitions, five as the prime contractor and two as a subcontractor. The benefits of converting customers to multi-year contracts were enormous. The new contracts were much larger, and the company formed several lasting strategic teaming relationships. As if that weren't enough, the portfolio of multi-year contracts was valued highly, especially by companies whose objective was to penetrate the Navy market.

Examine your company's current customer and contract mix. What needs and characteristics do your customers share? Who competes with you in that market space? Is the market for your products and services expanding or contracting? What is your market share, and what actions are you taking today to acquire a larger share? If you can't give precise answers to these questions, you may have a scattered customer base—it could be a mile wide and an inch deep. The most likely buyers for your business will be companies that want to enter or expand their presence in your market. Today is the ideal time to start implementing a strategy that focuses your customer and contract portfolio in high-growth areas, and eliminates one-of-a-kind and low-margin customers.

In general, a small number of loyal customers have a higher value to potential buyers, as long as no single customer represents more than 20 percent of your annual revenue. Furthermore, prime contracts are valued significantly higher than subcontracts because buyers want to control the customer relationship. Similarly, the market value of contracts that are difficult to transition to a new owner is low. A focused customer base will have special appeal to strategic buyers who are looking to penetrate your market, and financial buyers who plan to use your company as a platform for a roll-up. That base also will appeal to strategic buyers who are attracted to your intellectual property, and to lifestyle buyers whose objective is to run a company like yours on a day-by-day basis.

MISTAKE #14

LOOKING LIKE
EVERYBODY ELSE

Your **brand** *communicates purpose to customers
and employees, differentiates you from competitors,
and makes your company worth more to a buyer.*

Agovernment services firm in Washington D.C. branded itself as the *Project Management Company*. The truth is that hundreds of companies within twenty-five miles of the Capital routinely provide project management services to government agencies, many of them as effectively and some at lower cost. But this company has clearly communicated to customers and employees that its corporate purpose is *project management*. When a government agency needs project management services, this company is among the first they think of.

Their clear brand also attracts employees whose goal is to be project managers. They instill project management in the culture by requiring employees to become certified as project managers, by having a written methodology and extensive tools, by creating project management sub-specialties, and by offering a wide range of project management training courses. Employees know the company's brand and their individual role in its strategy. The company accelerated its growth by linking its brand with customer and employee needs. A few years ago, the company was sold for a very favorable multiplier.

Customers, employees, and buyers are drawn to companies that have clear and relevant branding. In fiercely competitive industries, branding is as important to success for start-up businesses as it is for Fortune-500 companies. One form of branding is your intellectual property—use it to distinguish your company from its competitors. Branding builds lasting customer and employee bonds as surely as do superior service, quality products, and generous benefits. Companies that communicate their brand effectively in the marketplace create more real and perceived value than their competitors, and retain their customers longer.

What you do, how you do it, and *the results your company produces for customers* are intellectual property—the essence of your company's brand. Once your brand is clear, communicate it to customers and employees through multiple channels including:

- Active participation in relevant associations
- Articles in industry-leading periodicals
- Seminars, workshops, and published books
- Corporate certifications (e.g., CMMI)
- Trademarks, logos, patents, and other intellectual property
- Attractive and informative marketing materials
- A proactive presence on the web (not just a website)

Use several of these techniques in tandem to differentiate your company from competitors. Don't look like everybody else! Buyers will pay a premium to acquire a company that is well-known and well-regarded because such a company has a competitive edge in the market.

In today's global economy, like previous times, the more you please customers, the more they will buy and refer new customers. Simple, yes; easy, no. Lacking a brand, you may find that your company is trying to do business with any customer who will pay you. But if your company delivers a product or service that is perceived in the market as unique and superior to other choices, you have a clear advantage. Furthermore, if you deliver that product or service using unique tools or a proprietary process that is hard to duplicate, that intellectual property is worth even more to a buyer.

How can you tell if your company has a brand that is recognized by customers and competitors? Ask yourself the following ten questions to assess the strength of your company's brand:

1. Do my customers believe they get something from my company that they can't get anywhere else?
2. Do customers buy from my company with full confidence in the quality and utility of the products and services they will receive?
3. Do customers often switch from competing businesses to buy from my company?

4. Are customers willing to pay a premium price to purchase my company's offerings over competing alternatives?

5. Do customers return again and again for follow-on purchases without advertising and discounts?

6. Do my customers and suppliers routinely refer other customers because they have received excellent service?

7. Have my revenue, margins, and profits increased annually for at least the last three consecutive years?

8. Does my sales volume increase even when prices increase?

9. Is my company known for using unique processes or tools to produce the products and services we sell?

10. Are my company and my employees frequently cited in well-known industry publications?

If you answered eight or more questions *yes*, your company has a strong brand. If you had five to seven *yes*es, you are well along the path toward building a recognized brand. If you had less than five *yes*es, then you have work to do to distinguish your company from its competitors.

When you sell your company, you won't be paid explicitly for your brand. Instead, its economic value will show up as a revenue multiplier that is on the high end of industry averages. That being said, the value of your brand can be estimated. Its replacement value is the amount a new owner would have to pay for the trademarks, publicity, websites, logos, advertising, and marketing materials required to build the level of name recognition and customer loyalty that your company currently enjoys in the market.

Your brand also has an economic value that is related to how much more per year customers pay for your offerings than they would pay for your competitors' offerings. Increasing the value of your company when the time comes to sell it is a plus, of course, but the compelling reason to brand your company is that, without a brand, you will be challenged to produce profitable revenue growth year after year. So don't look like everybody else. Brand your company!

MISTAKE #15

DANCING WITH SUGAR PLUM FAIRIES

Don't delude yourself by expecting an outlandish price for your company. Check the market and know what it's really worth.

Dick admits to "dancing with the sugar plum fairies" for several years before selling his company. For example, he daydreamed about what he would do if his company sold for a 1.2 revenue multiple. A week later, he would read about a similar company that sold for a 1.4 multiple. Of course, a month later there would be a 0.8 multiple, but he would ignore that data point. He often laid awake in bed thinking about everything he would do with the proceeds: pay off the mortgage, establish a trust for his family, travel, and so on. He knew the industry-average multiples, but felt that his company was far above average.

Advisors suggested that he hire a Certified Valuation Expert (CVE) to find out the company's value. He did so, and in addition to knowing the value at one point in time, he learned the 17 factors (see Appendix) that determine value in a buyer's eyes. The CVE designed an algorithm using the factors to measure whether the value increased or decreased each month. The algorithm couldn't predict exactly what the company was worth since that depended on the buyer, but it did tell Dick if he was doing things that increased its value. In addition, Stuart became Dick's financial and tax advisor, and suggested tax-advantaged ways to invest the proceeds and protect them from creditors.

One of the first tasks in determining the value of your company is to restate its financial statements from the perspective of the buyer. You'll probably want help from your CPA to do so. You may think restating financial statements sounds like doctoring your records, but that's not what we mean. Most business owners deduct all allowable expenses to minimize taxes. When a business is offered for sale, however, the buyer will want to know how much cash the business will generate.

The first step is to prepare a *pro forma* income statement that begins with EBITDA (earnings before interest, taxes, depreciation, and amortization). Then adjust EBITDA by: (1) adding expenses the new owner will not incur (e.g., your salary and benefits), and (2) subtracting expenses the buyer must incur that you did not recognize. For example, if the buyer must hire someone to replace you, subtract a reasonable compensation package for that person. The adjusted earnings are how much disposable cash flow the business will produce for the buyer.

Most companies are valued as a multiple of their disposable cash flow, and adjusted earnings are a convenient way to determine that value. Each industry has a range of multiples that depend on market trends, capital requirements, return-on-investment, and other factors. A company with growing revenue and profit, loyal customers, a strong operations team, and a favorable reputation will be at the upper end of the range; while a company with low earnings, *ad hoc* procedures, and financial warts will be at the low end. The multiple that your company earns will reflect its attractiveness in terms of financial strength and the ease of the transition to a new owner.

The value of a business where the owner is a major player in daily operations (often called a "lifestyle business") is calculated differently, usually as a multiple of Seller's Discretionary Earnings (SDE). SDE starts with the company's EBITDA and then adds owner benefits, non-recurring expenses, and discretionary expenses a new owner may choose not to incur (e.g., luxury auto and club membership). The adjusted SDE shows how much cash the business produces annually for the benefit of the owner. Buyers generally pay one to four times SDE. Seller financing often justifies a higher multiple than all-cash deals.

Whether a deal is an equity sale or asset sale also affects price. The differences are complex and affect how the seller's proceeds are taxed and the deductibility of the buyer's payments. It also will determine if the liabilities are transferred to the new owner or retained by the seller. Sellers generally want an equity sale because of the favorable income tax treatment, and all liabilities remain with the entity unless explicitly excluded from the sale. However, the buyer pays the purchase price mostly in after-tax dollars. On the other hand, buyers prefer an asset sale where the seller retains the company's legal shell and sells its tangible assets (e.g., equipment, inventory, and contracts) and intangible assets (e.g., name, intellectual property, and processes) to the buyer, who integrates them into an existing or new company. The buyer is allowed to deduct most of the purchase price by amortizing or depreciating the difference between the asset costs and their purchase price. However, in an asset sale, the seller generally faces a high income tax liability.

The due diligence process in an equity sale is more complicated than in an asset sale. However, in some cases, an equity sale may be necessary for the buyer to claim the performance history of the acquired entity or to avoid the customers' rights to terminate contracts upon a sale. This is a big problem for government contractors.

There's yet another wrinkle: an IRC Section 338 election, which for tax purposes treats an equity sale as if assets were sold and the proceeds were distributed to the old owners. Buyers want the Section 338 election because it increases the tax basis of the assets and allows them to claim higher depreciation and amortization. Conversely, the election adversely affects sellers because part of the proceeds are taxed as ordinary income rather than capital gains. However, since the election benefits buyers, they usually will agree to increase the price if the seller agrees to join in the election. Please consult your CPA for a thorough discussion of how a Section 338 election might apply to selling your company.

While selling your business hopefully will provide financial security, recall the adage: "*A lucky man can make a $1,000,000, but a smart man can protect and grow $1,000,000.*" Consider two questions. First, how will you protect the proceeds from taxes and creditors? And second, if proceeds are more than you need in your lifetime, what is the most tax effective way to pass part of the proceeds to your heirs? Such financial planning should be completed before you begin the sale process.

If you plan to build another business rather than retire, then you must protect the sale proceeds from creditors in case your next business fails. Similarly, if you want family members to benefit from any proceeds that remain after your death, transfer part of your stock via a sale or gift to a family trust or partnership before the sale. For example, in selling Dick's business, Stuart formed a family partnership to establish a private annuity for the benefit of Dick and his wife. While the IRS has reduced the income tax benefits of such private annuities, they are still a useful tool for creditor protection.

Depending on your personal goals and financial position, there are several types of trusts that can be used, including a self-settled creditor-protected trust, a dynasty trust, a grantor-retained interest trust, among others. The rules governing such trusts are complex. Therefore, consult your attorney and CPA about this type of financial planning well before the sale of your business.

If your sale will generate a substantial income stream and you do not have family members to benefit from the proceeds, you might consider a charitable remainder trust to protect the proceeds and reduce taxes. In simple terms, a person who creates a charitable remainder trust transfers property to the trust, and the trust distributes income from the property for either a fixed number of years (up to twenty) or for the life of one or two individuals. At the end of the period, the charity designated in the trust receives any remaining assets. The person who establishes the trust receives a current-year deduction for the value of the remainder. As for other types of trusts, the rules that govern charitable remainder trusts are complex, so consult your attorney and CPA about this type of planning.

Finally, if you are planning to sell your company to employees, you may want to consider an Employee Stock Ownership Plan (ESOP). An ESOP will allow you to sell all of your business at one time or stage the sale over several years while deferring recognition of the gain on the sale. IRS rules regarding ESOPs are complex, so implement an ESOP only with counsel from an ESOP specialist. In addition, the annual costs of administering an ESOP are high. Therefore, an ESOP is a practical strategy only when sale proceeds are expected to exceed $10 million.

In closing, when: (1) you know the value of your company, (2) that value exceeds what you need to fund your exit, and (3) the market is willing to pay that price, then you can exit! Chapter 3 (Mistakes #25 through #39) provides guidance on how to conduct the sale transaction. Chapter 2 (Mistakes #16 to #24) discusses actions that a buyer should be taking to prepare for a purchase while you were preparing for a sale.

CHAPTER TWO

PREPARING FOR A DEAL
AS THE BUYER

Acquisition isn't a growth strategy in itself. Rather, it is one of several techniques you might use to expand your market share and build your company's capabilities.

After growing 25 percent or more for seven consecutive years, a company with $45 million in revenue had to upgrade its capabilities to compete with larger companies in its market. The infrastructure hadn't kept up with the growth, so the company experienced weaknesses like:

- A business development program that depended on a few stars
- An aging accounting system that was incapable of supporting the transaction volume and reporting requirements of a large company
- Human resource functions supervised by the office manager
- Lack of reliable internal financial reporting and control mechanisms

These challenges pushed the company's owner out of his comfort zone. At first, he considered selling the company, but instead decided to build their capabilities and infrastructure through an acquisition.

He hired an investment banker to identify targets and received advice from the attorney and accountant who had helped the company since its inception. After a year-long acquisition, he closed a deal to buy a company with $15 million revenue, loyal customers, congruent capabilities, and an efficient accounting system. With $60 million revenue and twice the infrastructure, he thought his problems were over...in fact they were just beginning.

The combined business development and proposal writing workload was overwhelming. Glitches in invoicing and collections strained cash flow and caused the company to be late with payments to the bank. The acquired company's accounting system and procedures did not scale to support a $60 million company, and 20 percent of the seller's staff left because their benefits were not as good as the old benefits. Clearly, this company was not ready to undertake an acquisition and should have invested in infrastructure and organic growth before doing one.

Acquisition should not be a fix-it strategy or a way to employ excess credit or cash. Rather, it is a buy-versus-build alternative to organic growth as a way to achieve one or more of the following strategic goals:

- Diversify the business base horizontally or vertically
- Increase share or gain critical mass in existing markets
- Penetrate new customer segments or new geographic areas
- Access a new sales network
- Obtain new products or services to sell in current markets
- Gain access to new technologies or processes
- Extend the supply chain or eliminate a competitor
- Acquire key management personnel or sales staff
- Lower production costs through economies of scale

Which of these are priorities in your company's growth strategy? Growing organically is preferred because it is lower risk and more profitable than growth by acquisition—although it does take longer.

Acquisitions are risky business, and there is a significant chance that your acquisition won't meet its objectives. The most likely reasons why an acquisition might fail to meet its goals are that you:

- Acquired a business that is too far away from your core business, either technically or geographically
- Anticipated synergies that were unrealistic
- Have a weak system of internal governance and incentives
- Expected the acquisition to fix infrastructure weaknesses
- Stretched your financial and management capabilities too far
- Failed to design financial leverage into the deal (e.g., earn-outs)
- Became overly optimistic and overpaid in a hot market
- Didn't adequately plan for and invest in post-closing integration

And if that list isn't long enough to scare you into approaching an acquisition cautiously, consider these additional pitfalls:

- Cultural differences may lead to high turnover and other issues.

- The quality of service delivered by the combined entity could fall and lead to a loss of customers.
- Lower profit margins may result from duplicative capabilities.
- Lower revenue may result from a sales staff unable to cross-sell.
- Incompatible technologies may be difficult to integrate.
- Changes may occur in the economy or the market after closing.

Generally, consider an acquisition to be a failure if, two years after the closing, your revenue and profits have grown less than they would have otherwise. Acquisitions are not a panacea for growth. In fact, they often are a source of a whole new set of challenges.

The goal of an acquisition, of course, is to increase your competitive advantage by gaining new capabilities, new customers, and more resources. Returns-on-investment vary widely, so be coldly realistic in assessing an acquisition. Choose your target wisely, avoid overpaying, be conservative in estimating savings, don't take anything for granted in due diligence, and don't be afraid to walk away if the deal isn't a solid financial bet. And, after closing the deal, invest to achieve the gains you documented in your written acquisition plan. Acquisitions are definitely a *buyer beware* endeavor!

The M&A market swings like a pendulum from a buyer's market to a seller's market. Your decision to enter a market should be based on a strategic plan that uses acquisitions to boost organic growth. When the market is cool, companies with valuable capabilities and customers are available under favorable prices. On the other hand, in a hot market, you are likely to pay more for the same capabilities and customers. Planning ends and execution begins when your company is ready to invest the time and resources required to conduct and close an acquisition in accordance with your strategic plan.

This section discusses common mistakes that business owners make in rushing into acquisitions before their company is prepared. If you are serious about growing by acquiring another company, when you finish reading this chapter, it is likely that you will have a list of action items to do before you begin to undertake an acquisition transaction.

MISTAKE #16

NO STRATEGY FOR GROWTH

*Organic growth, coupled with acquisitions that accelerate
and complement organic growth, builds street value quickly.*

A new government services company was created in January 1996 when a New York-based investment firm paid $40 million to acquire a division of a large company with $109 million in annual revenue. The previous owner thought the division was too small to survive in an industry dominated by massive companies. The president of the new company was very clear that his "aggressive, but achievable" strategy to triple the company's revenue in three years was through organic growth augmented by an occasional strategic acquisition.

No mistakes were made here. The president said: *"Organic growth confirms that a company is delivering quality services to its customers, and enables it to sustain its business base and win new business."* The company consistently had high annual organic growth, and was widely recognized for its outstanding strategic planning capabilities. Its five-year organic growth plan targeted individual federal agencies and programs as must-wins. Companies who were seen as competitors for a must-win opportunity were approached either as a strategic bidding partner, or as an acquisition target.

The company's first year ended with 30 percent growth even though no acquisitions were completed, and that growth compounded in later years. During the second and third years, two acquisitions were closed for roughly $65 million in revenue, and the company's overall annual revenue grew to $542 million. In its first seven years, the company sustained its organic growth, and also closed a total of five acquisitions. It completed an Initial Public Offering (IPO) in March 2002, and was sold to a large defense firm for $2.2 billion in March 2006. This company's meteoric rise confirms the value of strategic planning that produces consistent organic growth, and the brilliant use of acquisitions to augment and accelerate that growth.

Strategic planning has fallen in and out of favor over the past several years. Some executives argue that the world of business changes so fast that the plans are irrelevant before they're even printed. Others refuse to do strategic planning because it's too hard to deal with complex, intertwined issues in a globally-connected world. We believe that strategic planning is even more essential when things change rapidly because it forces disciplined thinking, which is crucial in planning and executing an acquisition. We acknowledge that the business environment changes constantly, but that only means that time frames must be shortened and strategic plans must updated frequently. Do you have a written strategic plan that maps the path forward in your company's growth?

One key aspect of a growth strategy is whether your growth will be horizontal or vertical. Acquisitions can play a vital role in either choice. A horizontal acquisition is buying a company that offers services and products similar to yours, but to a different customer base. Conversely, a vertical acquisition is buying a distributor, supplier, or another company that offers value-added services or products to your current customer base. We recommend that your strategy specify either horizontal or vertical growth (but not both) because the risk of failure increases dramatically when you attempt to grow too fast and in different directions.

Your strategic plan should specify strategic objectives, quantitative goals, time frames, market assumptions, and resource requirements. We recommend that your goals be stated in terms of organic growth, with acquisitions being a way to achieve the organic growth rather than being the source of growth itself. At the end of the strategic planning session, the executive team should agree on acquisition criteria that support the company's strategic goals. The criteria should be written down, along with the assumptions and logic behind them. Don't be tempted to define criteria in terms of target companies that you already have in mind. One common characteristic among failed acquisitions is that the acquisition target was selected first and then justified after the fact.

The most successful acquisitions will deliver the customer access, new products and services, special skills, emerging technologies, and other resources necessary to achieve your organic growth objectives. Too often acquisition targets are defined in terms of annual revenue, EBITDA, and growth rate. But those financial characteristics determine what a company is worth, not whether it's a desirable target. A majority of an acquisition candidate's revenue should lie in areas directly related to your organic growth goals. The strength of the target's management team in the organic growth area (e.g., their relationships with potential new customers) also is a valuable characteristic of an ideal acquisition candidate.

The organic approach to growth requires innovations in your current product and service lines, superior customer service, and penetration of new markets. The challenge of organic growth, particularly for publicly-traded companies, is that it tends to be a slow process; 15 percent year-over-year organic growth is considered excellent, and many companies would be delighted with a 10 percent annual organic growth rate.

Furthermore, the extraordinarily rapid rate-of-change in today's globally-connected business world is another challenge to organic growth. Large industries (e.g., the automotive industry) can be redefined in the span of a year, and brand new industries (e.g., green technologies) can emerge just as quickly. Therefore, the slow pace of organic growth sometimes must be augmented with other ways to exploit changing markets. Acquisition is only one such technique; strategic alliances and intrapreneurship (i.e., internal ventures) are two other techniques. However, a lack of internal resources allocated to pursue and develop alliances and internal ventures often makes acquisition the most attractive approach to accelerate the organic growth specified in your strategic plan.

MISTAKE #17

ALL THAT GLITTERS
IS NOT GOLD

Spontaneous acquisitions rarely meet the buyer's expectations or achieve his strategic goals.

A CEO got a telephone call from a business acquaintance in another state. After a few minutes of small talk, the acquaintance asked directly, "*I'm retiring. Would you like the first shot at buying my company?*" His company provided similar services as the CEO's company, except the customers were commercial whereas the CEO's customers were mostly government. The CEO was excited by the high margins for commercial work, and the opportunity to stimulate his company's growth by quickly adding several million dollars in annual revenue.

The CEO cancelled his appointments, flew to the other state, and met with the acquaintance the following morning. Whirlwind negotiations were completed by the end of the day, and a Letter of Intent was signed by the end of the week. The CEO's Controller and Operations Vice President conducted a week of due diligence while the CEO lined up the financing. The lawyers took a few weeks to develop the Purchase & Sale Agreement, and the deal closed less than a month after that initial phone call.

The Operations Vice President temporarily moved to the other state to manage the new subsidiary. Unfortunately, because of the geographic separation and customer differences, there was little synergy between the two organizations. The acquired customer base stagnated, and profit and revenue declined. Two years later the CEO resold the company at a 40 percent loss. The glittering acquisition was anything but gold!

Without a strategic plan for growth that laid out specific criteria for an acquisition, any target seemed a glittering opportunity to this CEO. The opening section of Chapter 2 provided a list of strategic reasons why one company might acquire another. Fixing problems (e.g., slow growth or a weak management team) wasn't on the list because acquisitions often cause more problems than they fix.

In the best deals, buyers acquire a company that operates in related business areas. In the worst deals, targets are in distant areas. When the buyer and seller are different on more than one of the following factors, the acquisition is high risk:

- Similar customer base
- Same geographic region
- Compatible product and service offerings

We recommend you "stick to your knitting," since better knowledge of your target's markets, customers, products, and services usually means fewer unpleasant surprises, more synergy, and a realistic sale price. Acquisitions frequently fail because there was no synergy to begin with, or the expected synergy never materialized.

After the characteristics of an acquisition are documented in your strategic plan, designate members of the team who will lead the search-and-screen effort. The search team will need finance, accounting, legal, operations, and business development skills. Ideally, the team should be the same people who defined the original search criteria. If necessary, augment the search team with outside support such as an attorney, an investment banker, an accountant, and/or industry consultants.

The investment banker's role, whether he is an outsider or from the corporate development group, is to coordinate the identification and screening of target companies. The search will be conducted externally and internally. Externally, the banker will circulate acquisition criteria to brokers who handle deals in the industry. While this mass market approach usually produces multiple targets, it is public knowledge that those companies are for sale, and the most attractive targets probably will have already attracted the attention of other acquirers.

Internally, the search team will solicit suggestions for targets from business group managers. This proactive approach often will identify targets long before they enter the M&A market, and enable you to develop strategic alliances with them to pursue mutual opportunities. Those alliances allow you to build rapport with and evaluate the capabilities of a target company until such time as they are willing to be acquired—usually before their availability becomes public knowledge.

These days, obtaining information about target companies is easier than it used to be. The challenge is to correlate, validate, and evaluate the mountains of data available from the Internet and other sources—and to try to fill the information holes. The search team will determine if, and to what extent, each potential target meets the acquisition criteria set forth in the strategic plan and rank them by degree of fit. The ranking methodology you use should eliminate most of the targets; if it doesn't, the criteria were too loose to begin with.

Now the real fun begins: contacting the potential acquisition targets. The initial contact is usually made by a representative of the buyer or an intermediary in an off-the-record call to the target company's CEO. The scripted call should briefly describe your strategic objectives and how the target company could help you meet them. Starting with an informal communication allows the receiving CEO to consider the possibilities without a discoverable document that would require him to present the matter to the Board of Directors.

If the receiving CEO is receptive, the person making the call should provide further details about the inquiry, confirm any non-confidential business information about the target, and try to schedule a face-to-face meeting to discuss a potential transaction. Prior to such a meeting, it is appropriate to execute a Non-Disclosure Agreement (NDA) before exchanging sensitive information. Negotiating the Letter of Intent (LOI) is the next step, after which the detailed negotiations and due diligence begin as discussed in Chapters 3 and 4.

TIRE KICKING

Tire kicking is a huge waste of time for both buyers and sellers. Be sure you are committed to closing a deal, and be sure the sellers you meet are committed to selling.

An owner said he wanted to sell the business he had started over twenty years ago, and wondered how much information he should share in the courting phase, as opposed to the due diligence phase. He complained that he was tired of wasting time with wanna-be buyers who turned out to be tire kickers. He was concerned about protecting information from people who weren't serious buyers. Of course, we suggested that he ask a potential acquirer to sign a Non-Disclosure Agreement (NDA) that bars them from disclosing the information to anyone else. The NDA not only protects his company legally, but it also helps eliminate tire kickers who are usually reluctant to sign written agreements.

In addition, we recommended that, very early in the discussions, the seller screen potential buyers with a set of questions. For example, ask them to:

- Describe their criteria for an ideal acquisition
- Specify the size of company they are prepared to buy
- Identify the source of funds for the acquisition
- Tell how long they have been searching for a target
- Describe other companies they have purchased

If a prospective buyer answers these questions candidly and completely, and is willing to sign the NDA, he probably is a serious buyer rather than a tire kicker. At that point, the discussions can include summary financial results and status, and proceed toward a Letter of Intent (LOI). However, in no case should the seller expose his financial records and proprietary processes to a buyer until the LOI is signed and due diligence begins.

Dick acknowledges being a tire kicker in his two attempts to buy a company. Results speak for themselves: He never signed an LOI which, of course, means he never closed a deal as a buyer even though he spent hours of his own time, his management teams' time, and an investment banker's time. In both cases, he developed written criteria, retained an investment banker, and reviewed more than a dozen target companies. But an acquisition was not in his DNA; he was afraid of the financial risks involved, and backed away from every deal. Dick wishes he hadn't wasted his company's time and money when he wasn't psychologically prepared to do a transaction.

On the other side of the transaction, Dick ran into several types of tire-kicking buyers when it was time to sell his company. He routinely received three to five calls each month asking if he wanted to sell his company. At first, he responded to most of them. But very quickly he found that most calls were from brokers looking for a new client or companies trying to lure him into attending a seminar. He actually participated in one of the seminars and came away convinced it was time to sell, and he should list his company with the broker who ran the seminar. However, he inquired about the broker's firm through his CEO peer group and found that their track record was abysmal.

There are several traps that buyers fall into which point to tire kickers. Given that you're reading this book, we expect that you are not a tire kicker. That being said, however, it might be interesting to see if you recognize any of the following characteristics in your approach to buying a company:

- *Bargain Hunters* are looking for a business in distress, one where the seller is facing a crisis and might be willing to sell his company below market value in return for a quick closing.
- *Window Shoppers* evaluate dozens of businesses but are not ready emotionally or financially to buy one. They lack urgency and are more curious about the process than committed to closing a deal.
- *Penniless Shoppers* really would like to buy a business, but when it comes time to commit the cash, they are either unwilling or unable to come up with large sums of personal or borrowed money.
- *Comparison Shoppers* use the premise of buying a business to gain sensitive information about customers, competitors, and suppliers. They aren't really interested in buying a business at all.
- *Aimless Shoppers* have the resources to complete a deal, but don't really know what they are looking for. They look at businesses of any

size in their industry, but never find one that is exactly right.

Committed buyers know exactly what they want. They are able to screen a large number of target businesses and quickly determine which, if any, fit their strategic criteria.

Tire kicking can hurt a buyer in several ways. For example, the buyer's staff may be concerned that a potent acquisition could adversely impact their jobs. That uncertainty can lead to higher turnover and affect the buyer's profitability and ability to finance a future acquisition. It is important for both buyers and the sellers to hold M&A plans close to the vest until they are relatively sure that the transaction will close.

Being a committed buyer means that you willingly accept the:

- Transaction costs including price, legal and accounting expenses, post-closing investments, and key people retention agreements.
- Lower productivity and availability of your accounting, business development, operations, and legal teams during the negotiations and due diligence process.
- Doubts and fears, ambiguities, surprises, and risks that any given transaction might not work, despite everyone's best efforts!

If you are ready to go into debt, fork over a pile of money, and begin to run a company that, in reality, you know almost nothing about, then you are not a tire kicker.

MISTAKE #19

WHERE'S THE MONEY?

You can't lock in financing too early. Also be sure your
banker knows what to expect—bankers don't like surprises!

The buyer evaluated two years of audited financial statements for the target company—they were outstanding. He took those statements and the current-year July statements to his banker and received preliminary approval for the loan. Financial, operational, human resource, and legal due diligence were going well, and everything seemed to be on track for the scheduled December 31st closing.

Then came October's financial statements, which were awful! There was a loss and the cash position deteriorated. What went wrong? Seems the company, a subchapter-S corporation that filed cash-basis taxes, had begun its regular year-end tax-reduction actions. They purchased extra inventory and supplies, paid subcontractors and other payables, granted bonuses, and deferred collections. The seller was reducing income taxes in case the deal didn't close, just like he had done in previous years. For the same reasons, November's statements were even worse.

The buyer took the statements to his banker and explained what had happened. Surprised, the banker said he understood but nevertheless cut the loan ceiling. The buyer asked the seller to make up the shortfall with seller financing, but the seller refused since he wasn't comfortable with the security the buyer offered. The deal died. Obviously, the buyer should have locked in the loan based on July's statements, and told the banker to anticipate end-of-year tax planning adjustments by the owner.

In another case, a $4 million company won a competitive auction to purchase a $20 million company. Thinking big, the buyer had lined-up financing through a bank loan, two outside investors, and his own cash. The bank loan was contingent on investments by the buyer and the two investors. When one of the investors withdrew, the bank reduced the loan ceiling and the buyer was forced to request seller financing. At first the seller agreed, but later backed out of the negotiations and accepted a lower price from a buyer who didn't need seller financing. These stories provide two lessons: (1) you can't lock in financing too early, and (2) always tell your banker what to expect—bankers don't like surprises!

Financing often is the most creative aspect of an M&A transaction. Acquisitions can be funded through a combination of sources including:

- *Internal Cash.* How much can you afford to invest from your own personal funds and from your company's cash reserves?
- *Bank Loans.* What is the maximum loan a bank will approve for a given size transaction, and under what interest rate and covenants?
- *Outside Investors.* How much would they invest in an acquisition, and in return for what ownership percentage or interest rate?
- *Your Company's Stock.* How much is it worth per share, and how much ownership dilution are you willing to absorb?
- *Seller Financing.* As a last resort, how much will you need?

It is best to arrange financing *before* you begin contacting sellers. First determine how much cash you will need for the acquisition and post-closing cash flow. Start developing a *pro forma* balance sheet and income statement by combining your financials and the financials for a hypothetical target. If you'll need funds other than from your company and yourself, use the *pro forma* financials to solicit loans from bankers and backing from investors. Visit your banker and ask: "*Hypothetically, if I bought a business whose financials were like these and combined financials looked like these, would you lend us $X million and under what terms?*" Get the banker's response in writing. Work with multiple banks because loan terms vary. In general, it's easier to negotiate with a banker hypothetically. If they aren't willing to grant the loan, they'll tell you how much more outside equity you must secure to get the loan.

Small Business Administration (SBA) and other government loans can be excellent financing sources. Banks prefer SBA loans because they reduce the bank's risk, which allows them to offer more favorable interest rates. However, government loan programs have long approval lead times, and place restrictions on how funds are paid to the seller. Also, some banks have more experience than others with the SBA. A naïve banker may be surprised when a government administrator tells you both about a new restriction. Nothing will sour a deal faster than asking the seller to renegotiate terms because of new loan restrictions.

Since the 2007–8 financial crisis, bankers are more conservative than ever. One banker said: *"The wild, wild west days of M&A are gone, but I'll approve a loan for a buyer who finances half of the deal from his balance sheet."* Bankers prefer to hear from you before you negotiate with a seller. Supported by *pro forma* financial statements, they usually look for a five-year payback from current cash flow and a debt-to-equity ratio of four to six (previously, the max was eight). They also look for a debt coverage ratio of 1.25 to 1.5. Experience in the industry where you are acquiring is also vital. Financial management experience is valued more highly than operational experience, and experience dealing with market downturns can be a big plus.

Caution: loan approval from a bank can take months. Also, beware of banks that are financially troubled or are in the process of their own M&A transaction because lending criteria may change without warning. If your purchase agreement specifies a closing date, you may jeopardize closing by waiting too long to submit loan paperwork. If your LOI has a financing contingency, make sure the contingency clock doesn't start to run until the seller delivers all data that the bank needs. We recommend adding a provision in the purchase contract to automatically extend closing if the bank fails to process and approve the loan in a timely way.

Partial seller financing is common in small transactions. Terms of the promissory note can be a source of heated negotiations because the seller will be concerned about your ability to pay down the seller's loan. The seller's security terms may become onerous if he thinks that your plans for the business endanger its financial condition. All in all, it is risky to depend on seller financing to close a deal.

No matter what combination of sources you use to finance your deal, start grooming your financial statements today. Ask a CPA to compare your company's financial strength to industry-standard ratios like the current ratio, debt-to-equity ratio, interest coverage, and working capital. Have your CPA recommend actions to improve these ratios and increase your company's ability to leverage its assets in an acquisition.

LIVE BY THE SWORD, DIE BY THE SWORD

Roll-up is a growth strategy that uses serial acquisitions to take advantage of higher price multiples for larger companies.

Having reached $20 million annual revenue through organic growth, a pure-play government services chose to accelerate its growth through roll-ups during the early 2000s. Their strategic plan was to buy companies that delivered services to federal agencies, integrate them, and take the combined company public. In two years, they closed three acquisitions that pushed revenue past $100 million. After taking a year to integrate their operations, the company went public in 2002 at $156 million in annual revenue. But they weren't done yet!

With a treasure chest from the IPO, they upped the ante by acquiring reasonably-priced larger companies. Like a snake digesting a calf, each time they bought a company they paused to assimilate its operations before swallowing the next acquisition. The president said: *"We didn't go after every acquisition we saw, and didn't close every one we went after. Some we lost and we backed away from others because something came to light during due diligence. Of the acquisitions we pursued, we closed less than half."* They examined a constant stream of potential acquisitions and, at one point, closed two deals in a single month.

However, operating in the quarterly cycle of the public market, they could not afford to pause between deals to resolve issues. By growing rapidly, they became a darling of Wall Street and were hard-pressed to control Wall Street's expectations. Since operations and acquisitions consumed current cash flow, when top-line growth slowed they had to reduce spending. Braking is always harder than acceleration.

They were not trying to be acquired—but the market got tough. Like others in the industry, their annual organic growth fell under 10 percent. When they received unsolicited offers at a substantial premium over the current trading price, the Board had to take them seriously. In 2008 with revenue near $600 million, the company was sold to a subsidiary of a British corporation for about $510 million. Live by the sword and die by the sword. You can't always dictate when you will go public, and once you go public, you lose some control over when you will get bought.

Roll-up as an acquisition strategy is a financial decision. Since the price multiplier is higher for a larger company in most industries (the *size premium*), building revenue through multiple acquisitions has a built-in return-on-investment. For example, a private-equity roll-up in IT security used a commonwealth approach which allowed acquired companies to retain autonomy and manage their contracts with oversight from headquarters. The equity firm pays three to five times EBITDA to buy companies in the government IT sector, and expects to sell the company at six or seven times EBITDA.

Roll-ups are common today in green technologies, physical security, cyber-security, education, and health care, for example. Success breeds success in the roll-up market. If that's your growth strategy, best to start small. Don't go for a home run in your first acquisition and risk striking out. Better to establish a track record for success that attracts sellers and bankers to future deals. "*Nothing sells quicker than success.*" Therefore it is important that your first acquisition be successful, or you will limit your ability to do future transactions. Besides, smaller companies are easier to integrate and pose less financial risk than mega-acquisitions.

A caution to public companies: Wall Street's insatiable expectations for revenue and earnings growth often cause M&A addictions. But growth comes in only two flavors: organic and acquisitions. In most industries, organic growth is a modest number that cannot be easily increased. That means acquisitions must fill the gap between revenue and earnings targets and the organic growth that your core business can deliver. The result is your M&A staff must produce an ever-increasing amount of growth each year. This is a risky strategy because it focuses on revenue and profit growth, rather than on building a fundamentally sound business. Maybe renewed focus on organic growth would ensure that your company doesn't die by the same sword that fuels its growth.

HIRING JACK THE RIPPER

The experience and chemistry of your acquisition advisors are equally important. The wrong advisors will not only wreck an acquisition, they can damage your company's reputation.

A company's three-year business strategy called for development of a new product line and acquisition of a business to help roll it out to a broad customer base. The owner asked the company's CPA and attorney to jointly direct the M&A effort. Neither had much M&A experience, but the owner trusted them because they had served his company for more than ten years. Together, the CPA and attorney interviewed and selected an investment banker to identify acquisition targets.

Thirteen candidate companies were found, but the screening process quickly eliminated eleven of them. The buyer's president met with the CEOs of the two remaining companies and selected the target company based on strategic alignment—even though the price was high. An LOI was signed, and the due diligence process began. In an effort to negotiate a lower price, the CPA was so aggressive in citing inadequacies in the seller's financial records and performance that the seller's CEO said, *"It felt like I was working with Jack the Ripper."* The deal ended abruptly after a shouting match between the CPA and the seller's CFO.

Your acquisition team must have experts with broad M&A expertise that you can trust to give you straight answers—but they also must have the right chemistry. The wrong advisers can kill your deal and hurt your company's reputation. M&A deals frequently begin with good rapport between the buyer and the seller, but that rapport can dissipate quickly in the heat of negotiations. When patience is wearing thin and tempers flare, you want a team that will calm the waters and use their ingenuity to make an impossible deal possible.

You can't be too careful in selecting your advisors; they will make or break your deal. Of course, you ultimately make all the decisions as the owner, but surround yourself with acquisition all-stars including:

- An investment banker who will help find and evaluate candidates, and take the lead during most of the negotiations
- An accountant/CPA who will lead financial due diligence, advise you on tax-advantaged ways to structure the deal, and work with your attorney and broker effectively
- A finance expert who will help arrange financing for the deal
- An attorney who will lead the legal and human resources parts of due diligence, work with your CPA to document a tax-advantaged deal, and prepare the purchase agreement and other documents
- An industry expert, usually an executive from your staff, who will evaluate the seller's customer base and product/service offerings

In some transactions, one expert can serve multiple roles. For example, with appropriate conflict-of-interest disclosures, Stuart has represented both the buyer and seller in several deals. This approach reduces costs and expedites closing because one professional prepares the documents with no back-and-forth between attorneys on boilerplate. The buyer and seller, if they desire, can engage other legal counsel to review particular provisions in the agreements that are of concern to them.

But which of your key advisers should you hire first? There are two approaches. First, if you have a trusted associate, such as a Board member, an executive, or a CPA or attorney who has M&A experience in your industry, that person may lead the acquisition team and help you select an investment banker. Second, if a trusted advisor isn't available, choose an investment banker yourself. We recommend approaching an investment banker first because he will usually direct the acquisition and coordinate the negotiations. In addition, an investment banker will know several accountants and attorneys who have been successful in transactions in your industry. Interview the candidates he recommends and pick advisors with whom you feel a rapport.

Many owners rely on the CPAs and attorneys who represented them in the past—which may or may not be wise. Obviously, an advisor who serves you well has your trust and understands your business and personal situations.

However, they may lack the expertise or personality to handle a complex acquisition. So you may be working with a stranger on the most important deal of your career. Interview thoroughly and hire carefully. Systematically evaluate the candidates' records:

- Are they thoroughly versed in the unique issues of your business?
- Have they represented other companies in your industry and closed those transactions successfully?
- Do they understand the tax laws involved in structuring your deal?
- Are they familiar with pricing issues, representations, earn-outs, and warranties that are common in your industry?
- Will they appear credible to the seller?

Take a long, hard look at your current advisers to decide if you will need more qualified advisors to guarantee that the deal will go through.

If you don't have a full-time acquisition specialist on your staff, you will probably need to hire an investment banker to direct the search and screening process. Investment bankers often are in contact with owners who have expressed a desire to sell. Buyers are at a disadvantage in such cases because parameters of the sale have already been determined. For example, sellers choose a time to sell, the asking price, and the payment terms. A buyer can only respond. However, that doesn't mean you are at the mercy of a seller. At times, a buyer can initiate the inquiry to a seller who has not publicly announced an intention to sell. Investment bankers know how to conduct such inquiries and create seller interest when none had existed. We recommend that you provide written acquisition criteria to several investment bankers, interview them, and select the one who understands your objectives and has a clear plan to find candidates.

Most growing companies lack the internal resources that a Fortune-1000 company can apply to an acquisition. So it is essential for them to recruit advisors to augment the availability and expertise of their staff. Some companies use a "war room" to conduct acquisition meetings and store confidential data. They find a war room helps communications and stimulates a feeling of shared purpose, especially among executives who manage acquisitions in parallel with other corporate functions. Even so, small companies can compete favorably with large companies in the acquisition arena by training executives in M&A processes and hiring experts on a retainer basis—avoiding the Jack the Rippers, of course!

MISTAKE #22

IMPATIENCE

Acquisition is an important task—but not an urgent one.
Be patient in the search for the perfect candidate because
that patience will pay huge dividends in the long run.

Dick's acquisition efforts were unsuccessful primarily because of his impatience. He developed a wish list of precise criteria for the perfect acquisition target, hired an investment banker, and gave the list to him. Using his industry contacts and research department, the investment banker came up with a so-called long-list of eight candidates in about a month. Next, the banker worked with Dick's staff to develop questions in three areas to determine the target's:

(1) Willingness and expectations relative to being acquired

(2) Annual revenue relative to the size of an ideal target

(3) Customer base and offerings to identify potential synergies

The purpose of the questions was to solicit the information required to reduce the long list to a short list of one or two target companies.

For a variety of reasons, none of the eight candidates met all of the criteria. But, in a hurry to show progress to the Board, Dick picked the two best, and the investment banker contacted them by phone. One company wasn't interested in being acquired, and the other provided interesting answers. To shorten a long story, after a month of intense phone conversations and a series of face-to-face meetings, both sides agreed there wasn't a good match, and a Letter of Intent was never started. The investment banker resumed the search for candidates, but Dick's acquisition effort fizzled. He had wasted a considerable amount of money to hire the investment banker and many hours of management time, not to mention the opportunity cost of how that time and money might have been spent to grow the company organically.

The investment banker, in this case an outsider, did exactly what he was hired to do: He developed a long-list of acquisition targets. Working with other brokers, he identified five companies who had declared their intention to be acquired. He also searched and found three companies who met the criteria, but had not yet announced a desire to be acquired. The corporate development group often performs these tasks in large companies.

Broad market queries usually produce candidates, but in most cases, those companies are either involved in a limited auction or already have attracted attention from other acquirers. The best acquisition targets are frequently found through research or suggestions from line managers. Such proactive search methods identify targets well before they enter the M&A market. Even if a company is not interested in being acquired *today*, they could become an excellent strategic partner—and *tomorrow* they may change their mind about being acquired. Generally, a majority of the candidates on the long-list will be companies who have officially entered the M&A arena.

In the age of the Internet, getting information about target companies is a little easier. Even many small companies use websites to publicize their product and service offerings, list their major customers, and give background information on their executives—the answers to question (3) above. Some sites compile media articles about the company on their website, and even provide information about the company's origin, size, and growth rate. Your search team should surf the web and sift through the heaps of data provided from the Internet and other sources in order to determine if and to what extent a company meets the criteria defined in your strategic plan and acquisition wish list.

However, the Internet won't answer all your questions. Most of the missing information must be obtained from the source: the company's owner and senior executives. The investment banker often will make the initial contact with a potential acquisition target via a phone call to the CEO or CFO. If the company is receptive after the first call, you should make a follow-up call a few days later.

The call would begin with a brief description of your strategic goals, why you think the target company might help you meet such objectives, and the advantages that your company offers to their company. Best practice is to use a prepared script for the follow-up phone call. You may want to incorporate one or more of the following lines of questioning into the script as appropriate to your industry:

- We understand you may be interested in selling your company. Is that true? (Of course, if the answer is NO, the questions are over.)
- What would you want from a sale transaction? (Objectives? Cash? What multiplier? Timing? Stay or leave? Other?)
- What is your corporate ownership structure? How many owners?
- Identify the characteristics of an ideal buyer for your company.
- What was revenue and EBITDA in the trailing twelve months?
- Who are your best customers? How long have they been with you?
- What are your most lucrative product and service offerings?

Write down the answers you would expect to hear from a perfect target. Assuming the question-and-answer session goes well, the purpose of the phone conversation is to schedule a face-to-face meeting to discuss a potential deal. If that meeting occurs and both parties want to move to the next phase, it is appropriate to execute a Non-Disclosure Agreement (NDA) before exchanging sensitive business information.

Exercise the patience to say *NO* to all of the potential sellers on the long-list if none of them fully meet your criteria. Keep looking. You'll know in your gut when you find the right one: You'll be excited. You'll want to share the news with your Board members and senior staff. You won't have any doubt that this candidate is exactly the right one! (Don't be surprised, however, when such doubts show their ugly heads later in the process.) Furthermore, it may be that one of the candidates to whom you say *NO* today because of minor issues will become a viable candidate a year or more in the future. In any case, waiting for the ideal candidate will greatly increase your return on investment for the time and money you risk in the acquisition effort.

MISTAKE #23

ABANDONING YOUR PRICING STRATEGY

To succeed as a buyer, define a pricing strategy like Goldilocks' porridge: not too hot and not too cold—and then stick to it!

A company that averages one acquisition per year has a conservative and precise strategy for pricing that involves three steps. First, any acquisition must be accretive to earnings immediately. Second, offers are based solely on the intrinsic value: The internal rate-of-return when the target's projected EBITDA is evaluated against capital, income tax benefits, and transaction costs. And third, synergy is never included in an offer. Commenting on giving no value to synergy, the M&A boss said: *"Our long experience is that synergies don't happen most of the time."* Using this pricing strategy, the company has closed seven of the fourteen acquisitions it pursued in the last eight years.

Despite its conservative pricing strategy, the company found that it still overpaid on one occasion. The M&A boss said: *"I'll stick with our strategy— six out of seven is better than most!"* In that acquisition, the seller had a diverse range of customers in a high-growth sector; their customer base was "a mile wide and an inch deep" (see Mistake #13). The buyer's plan was to parley the seller's customer relationships into growth under its existing contract vehicles—but the growth never happened. The seller's customer base remained static after closing, and the acquisition did not meet the *pro forma* projections on which the purchase price was based.

Another company with an even more cautious pricing strategy had a different experience. They retained an investment banker, defined target characteristics, and lined up financing. But when they located the ideal candidate, they were unwilling to pay what the investment banker said was a fair market price. A year later, the target company was sold for 50 percent more than the price the investment banker recommended. What is a realistic price? Neither a buyer nor a seller knows because they are both emotionally involved in the deal. That's why you must define a pricing strategy before you evaluate a specific candidate.

Sometimes M&A markets are slow, and at other times they are hyperactive. Be especially careful during the hyperactive periods because buyers can get sucked into bidding wars with disastrous results. During the frenzy of a competitive bid, the price for a target can rise far above any justifiable level. The result is the "lucky" winner pays a premium that is virtually impossible to recoup—the so-called "winner's curse." After you apply your pre-set pricing strategy to determine a reasonable price for a target company, respect that price and don't bid significantly higher. It's all too common for a buyer who makes an acquisition during a hot market to regret the acquisition and wish they had patiently waited for a cooler market.

Consider two components in defining your pricing strategy: intrinsic value and synergistic value. Intrinsic value includes the value of a target company's assets, business operations, intellectual property, and cash flow irrespective of an acquisition. Synergistic value, on the other hand, assigns a dollar value to the revenue and profit increases that *may* occur after the two companies are merged. Calculations of intrinsic value are straightforward (assuming you forecast the market accurately) using recognized cost-of-money algorithms. Calculating the value of synergy, however, depends entirely on the assumptions you make about how the combined businesses will operate after closing. Such assumptions are unique to the companies involved in the deal, and the economies of scale may not be achievable.

If you consider it at all, the calculation of synergistic value might include financial benefits such as tax savings and cost-cutting, and/or operational benefits like cross-selling to each other's customer base and sharing strategic information. Since it is difficult to accurately forecast potential synergies that might occur in a given deal, if a significant part of the bid price is based on synergies, the most effective approach is to evaluate the merged entity as if it were an entirely new company.

Furthermore, post-closing integration investments are often needed to realize the projected synergies, and it is very difficult to accurately forecast the timetable for achieving such synergies. Investments may be required for:

- Facilities and systems consolidations
- Training for salesmen, customer support staff, and others
- New advertising and marketing initiatives

For example, technology investments may be required to achieve a free flow of sales, customer, and business information across the entire new enterprise. Such investments are in addition to the purchase price and transaction costs. Also, it's prudent to anticipate that other integration costs will be discovered during the due diligence process. Estimating these costs early in the transaction may affect the offering price.

At the end of negotiations, buyers usually pay a premium over the trading price (for public companies) or intrinsic value (for privately-held companies) of the target company in order to gain shareholder approval. But how much should that premium be? Buyers justify large premiums by convincing themselves that cost savings and cross-selling synergies will exceed the acquisition premium. Unfortunately, cost increases (not savings) often materialize after closing, and cultural mismatches can interfere with cross-selling possibilities. Earn-outs can be an effective mechanism to bridge the premium gap. Many experts say the #1 reason why buyers fail to achieve their financial goals in buying a business is poor strategic fit. Granting that that is correct, overpaying because of imaginary synergies is a very close second.

Pride has been called the worst of the seven deadly sins—and it's no stretch to put it at the top of the list of M&A evils as well. Just as pride is a fatal flaw in many Shakespearean heroes, so too can it become the downfall of executives who link their reputation to closing a deal. The pride of such acquisition-driven executives clouds their thinking and pushes them to submit outlandish bids. Even when they win the bid and close the deal, they find themselves buying an asset whose earnings will never cover the high premium they paid. We strongly recommend that you develop your pricing strategy before beginning to search for a candidate, and *stick to it* when you're bidding for a target that meets the acquisition criteria.

MISTAKE #24

FORCING IT DOWN THEIR THROATS

Involving line managers in the development of acquisition criteria substantially increases the return-on-investment.

In tracing the steady growth of a publicly-traded, multi-billion dollar company, it was no surprise to find that the company had prepared and followed a clearly defined growth strategy. What was a surprise was the important role that line managers played in forming and executing that strategy. Having reached the critical mass required to bid on the largest government contracts, the company's goal was to grow earnings 10 to 12 percent per year; revenue growth was ancillary. The earnings growth was produced primarily from organic growth, and the goals of the acquisition program were to complement the organic growth.

Each of the company's business groups defined annual growth goals and identified tactical gaps in their capabilities, technologies, customer base, and operating locations. Senior executives identified strategic gaps in the company's service offerings, and selected high-growth business sectors where building the company's market share was a strategic goal. The mission of the corporate M&A group was to fill those tactical and strategic gaps.

Occasionally a business group manager might identify a target, but no acquisition was pursued without the approval and active participation of the cognizant group manager. The Corporate M&A Director said: "*I can't imagine buying a company unless the line manager knew them intimately and endorsed the acquisition wholeheartedly.*"

On average, the company screens five candidates a month and closes one acquisition each year. When an acquisition candidate passes initial screening, it is referred to a line manager for evaluation. But there are no "force it down their throat" acquisitions; if the line manager says "*NO*," the acquisition ends. If the line manager likes what he sees, the M&A group signs the Non-Disclosure Agreement and begins to explore the target's financial performance in depth. The line manager oversees the operations portion of due diligence. When an acquisition is ready for approval by the Board of Directors, the line manager presents the business case, commits to a three-year profit and revenue forecast for the group, and describes the integration approach he intends to follow to achieve the projected results.

The forecast becomes the metric used to determine the acquisition's success and measure the line manager's performance. For example, in early 2007 at the peak of the market, the company offered the top price in a hotly competed bidding process. Despite the high price, the line manager was passionate about the target company and defended the acquisition vigorously at the Board meeting. The line manager beat the profit and revenue projections by over 10 percent in both of the first two years after the acquisition closed!

This approach produces consistent results because of the synergy it creates between the buyer's and the seller's managers during due diligence and integration. The post-closing organization should be structured in way that retains the seller's most competent people and puts them in positions with clear responsibilities. Furthermore, defining the new organization before closing gives both the buyer and the seller a clear picture of how things will operate after closing.

Line managers on the buyer and seller teams gain confidence in each other when they see how well they both understand the business and the rapport they have with customers. Buyers must minimize criticisms of the seller's managers and employees to avoid alienating them. Mutual confidence is more effective than employment agreements in retaining key people after closing. Merging the product/service delivery systems (including computer systems) that existed in both companies frequently requires an investment, which should be recognized as a transaction cost. Shared work ethics, a high level of operational excellence, and a clear commitment to quality bring the two teams together as one. These are key factors in the financial success of the merged group. Years of training and effective management are required to build a culture that produces quality products and services. In successful acquisitions, that culture is preserved and enhanced after closing.

CHAPTER THREE

GETTING THE DEAL
DONE AS THE SELLER

*Buckle your safety belt! You are about to begin the most
unpredictable race of your life—so you'll need a good pit crew.*

A seller insisted on using his own lawyer despite recommendations from his business broker. The broker had offered the names of three other lawyers who had M&A experience in the seller's industry. But the seller's attorney was a close personal friend who had represented him in business and personal matters for over twenty years. Since a customer is always right, the broker relented and made the best of the situation.

A month into the deal, the broker visited the lawyer for a meeting. When he arrived, the lawyer and his staff were reviewing law books to research the Bulk Sales Act, which applies to asset sales. One provision of the act requires the seller to notify creditors about the sale, a necessity that is usually met with an announcement in a newspaper at closing. But the lawyer insisted on mailing a registered letter to each of the two hundred firms and individuals who had been creditors of the company in the past twenty-four months. The lawyer's effort didn't sink the deal, but his costs were twice the usual fees for such a sale transaction—and most of the extra hours were spent on unimportant matters. The broker ended up picking up the slack and handled the core issues.

The type and amount of help you will require to sell your business depends on your answers to the following questions:

- Do you know who the buyer will be, or where to find buyers?
- Will you have time to participate actively in negotiations while simultaneously managing your company's daily operations?
- Are you effective at marketing your company to outsiders, making presentations, and negotiating complex contracts?

- Do you know what your business is worth?
- Do your attorney and CPA have significant M&A experience?

It also depends on the probable source of the buyer. For example, if you are selling to an insider (e.g., a partner or employee), you won't need a business broker. On the other hand, if you want an outside buyer, it's critical to retain a broker who will locate buyers you wouldn't find and act as an intermediary during negotiations. Since misunderstandings, divergent opinions, and personality conflicts occur in negotiations, it is helpful to have an intermediary like the broker who can save face by claiming that he misinterpreted or misrepresented your position.

Deciding who to retain on your team is a challenge for most sellers. But one thing is for sure: *Don't go it alone!* Depending on the nature of your sale, you will need one or more of the following professionals:

- An accountant is crucial to answer the seller's questions about how your company's financial statements and tax returns were prepared. Your regular CPA is suitable if he has experience in tax strategies and the tax implications of M&A transactions.
- A separate tax advisor will be necessary if your accountant isn't well-versed in M&A tax matters, if the deal involves complex tax issues, or if you need advice about: (1) investing sale proceeds in a tax-advantaged way, (2) creditor protection for sale proceeds, or (3) income, estate, and gift-tax planning.
- An attorney is essential to: (1) advise you regarding the business structure, ownership, contracts, leases, and employees; and (2) prepare/review documents such as Non-Disclosure Agreements, disclosure statements, Purchase & Sale Agreement, a consulting agreement, promissory notes, and escrow agreements. The attorney should have solid M&A experience in your industry. Also, unique expertise will be required if the transaction involves an Employee Stock Ownership Plan (ESOP).
- A business broker will be particularly valuable when you: (1) must maintain confidentiality about the sale, (2) need help finding and screening prospective buyers, (3) require someone to quarterback the transaction while you run your business, and (4) expect that the negotiations will get volatile and want to have an intermediary.

- A Certified Valuation Expert (CVE) is useful: (1) in planning your exit strategy, (2) to validate the price recommended by your broker, (3) in tax planning to develop an independent estimate of the company's value for the IRS, and (4) to provide a "fair value" opinion when the sale involves other shareholders or an ESOP.

Economists project that almost 20 percent of all businesses owned by baby-boomers will be offered for sale by the end of 2010 when the first boomers turn sixty-five years old. That projection means M&A experts will be busy, and buyers will have a variety of businesses to evaluate.

As a sale moves through the process, business owners get concerned about professional fees. When asked how much his fee will be, Stuart responds: *"I can tell you what it will cost to draft the documents, but I can't tell you what it will cost to complete the deal unless you can tell me when it will close and the M&A competence of the opposing counsel."*

CPAs, tax advisors, and lawyers generally provide M&A services on an hourly basis—and their fees grow quickly when a transaction drags on or goes off track. Valuation experts, on the other hand, deliver their expert opinion for a fixed price specified in an engagement letter. But business brokers are paid differently. Typically, they want earnest money when taking a deal (Dick paid $25,000 up-front) and a success fee payable at closing. The success fee is a percentage of the sale price, subject to a minimum fee—but brokers get paid nothing if the deal fails to close. It is good to have someone like the business broker pushing everyone to close when the others are getting paid by the hour.

This chapter covers the mistakes that sellers make in finding buyers, presenting the company to buyers, selecting the right buyer, negotiating the sale agreement, conducting due diligence, and closing the deal. As a seller, you must be concerned with all of these because any of them can blow up in your face; that's why you need an experienced team around you. According to Dealogic, of the deals announced publicly in 2008, 1,362 of them failed to close—the most ever. This chapter is intended to ensure that your deal doesn't become one of those statistics.

MISTAKE #25

SELLING YOURSELF SHORT

Buyers look for many things. So selling yourself short because of your small size or a few down years can be a costly mistake.

A CEO, facing his fiftieth birthday, reflected that he had started his telecommunications company when he was twenty-six years old. The business had provided a steady living for himself and his brother for a long time. He said he loved the rapid advances in applications and technology, he loved his employees, and he loved the customers *"most of the time."* But he was bored. He felt he wasted his abilities doing the same thing year-in and year-out for nearly half his life.

He considered selling the company, but with $3 million in revenue he thought it was too large to sell to a local competitor and too small to be sold to a national company. Besides, who would want a company that broke even last year and lost money the year before? Moreover, selling the company wouldn't give him enough money to retire anyway. He still wanted to work but didn't know what else he could do. On an emotional level, he was attached to what he had done for virtually his entire adult life and was scared to give it up.

For starters, we didn't agree that his business couldn't be sold. A business with stable cash flow in a growing industry can always be sold. He was blind when he thought the only buyers for his company were in the same industry. Buyers purchase other companies for many reasons, including some you couldn't even imagine. We told him that he was selling himself short, and that he should test the market.

He hired a business broker, who prepared a teaser and sent it to fifty-three companies; four the CEO suggested and forty-nine the broker identified. In six months, his company was sold to a publicly-traded company that wanted his customers and distribution network for a new product line. He was delighted with the price (0.8 multiplier on revenue) and ecstatic with his new position as VP of Sales for the mid-Atlantic region. Being an executive in a big company was just the challenge he needed!

Selling yourself short because you think your business is too small to attract attention from large companies can be a costly mistake that limits your exit options. The gap between your company's financial value and its market value can be substantial. The difference is intangible assets—in this case the company's customer base and distribution network.

About 40 percent of all privately-held businesses sold to U.S. public companies had annual revenue under $5 million and three-quarters had revenue under $25 million. If your company has a prime location that you own or control via a long-term, transferable lease; if you provide a service or product customers can't buy anywhere else; if customers are loyal to your service; if your company's name is widely recognized and you have had steady growth and profits, then your business will be very attractive to potential buyers— even the big guys!

Similarly, selling yourself short because of mediocre financial results is an equally big mistake. Strategic buyers look to the future. So a year or two of low profits or flat revenue may not affect the selling price, especially if the economy is down. The past is only one indicator of the future—and sometimes it's not a very good indicator. Getting a high multiple for your company depends more on the future than on today.

In analyzing your true financial position, look at the amount you take out of the business and year-end expenditures to reduce your income taxes. You may be granting yourself benefits a buyer wouldn't continue after purchasing your business. Such benefits are called owner add-backs. To determine your company's true financial value, prepare *a pro forma* financial statement excluding owner add-backs and expenditures you make solely for tax savings.

A word of caution: overselling can be just as damaging as selling yourself short. Buyers often pull the plug on deals when they feel they're being oversold with recent results that are unsustainable, or revenue and profit projections that are unrealistic and unsubstantiated. Mistake #12, *"Hockey Stick Projections,"* described a methodology for validating your projections of future revenue and profit. Buyers won't always agree with your projections, but that difference usually can be resolved through earn-outs and other variable payments.

MISTAKE #26

LIMITING YOUR POSSIBILITIES

*Offering your business for sale should be like the
coming-out party for a debutante—dress the business
in its finest and invite all the top suitors to the party.*

A business owner invested years in carefully preparing his company to be sold. He produced consistent 15–20 percent year-on-year growth for three years, increased margins each of the years, and developed accurate forecasts. Operating procedures were documented, and the staff worked together like a precision clock. His CPA and lawyer, both of whom had extensive experience in acquisitions, helped him groom the company. He was ready to sell the company—or so he thought!

Since he frequently responded to inquiries from subcontractors and competitors, he felt it would be easy to find a buyer and close a sale in four to six months. He kicked off the sale process by calling each of the people who had asked about buying his company. At first they seemed interested, and he met with them to discuss the possibilities. But one by one, each said *"NO."* He also put ads in two M&A websites and a trade journal, and received over twenty responses. Only one was a qualified buyer, but he was looking to buy a business in distress. Three months went by and he had not found a truly interested buyer.

Frustrated, he retained a business broker to locate a buyer. The broker said, *"You've been hiding your best stuff. Offering your business for sale is like a coming-out party for a debutante: dress the business in its finest and invite all of the top suitors to the party."* Working with the owner, the broker prepared a one-page teaser and a detailed selling memorandum. The teaser, which did not specify the company's name, was sent to a hundred suitors. Five months later, the business was sold to a foreign company that wanted to gain a foothold in U.S. markets through an acquisition. Without the broker, the seller had no way to know that such a buyer even existed.

Unless you plan to sell to an employee, partner, or family member, there's no way to know where your buyer will come from, why they're attracted to your company, or even why they want to buy a business in the first place. Your buyer might be a competitor, a supplier, a customer, an equity investor, or a foreign company. The buyer may be attracted to your location, your industry, your customers, your products or services, or your intellectual property. A buyer may be purchasing your business as a strategic addition to their existing company, as an investment that someone else will run, or for a personal reason like the desire to run his own business. Therefore, you must turn over as many rocks as soon as possible to find a buyer. A one-page teaser is a good starting place.

How long is a one-page teaser? You're right! But the challenge is to pack that page with juicy facts that entice buyers to take a closer look at your company. That single page must answer the following *what, when, where, who, why,* and *how much* questions for prospective buyers:

- What are you selling? Describe your business in a few sentences. For example: "A profitable CMMI level-3 software company with $9 million in revenue and a widely recognized reputation for secure systems and timely delivery."
- When was the company started? Either cite the founding date or how long the company's been in business. For example: "Since the company's founding in 1999, our CAGR has been 27 percent."
- Where is the company located? Describe the region in which the company operates in general terms: "We are located within eight miles of the Capitol Building in Washington, D.C. where federal agencies have their headquarters and central contracting shops."
- Who are your major customers? Describe your customer base in favorable economic terms: "Our federal government clients have increased their budget for secure computer systems by 68 percent over the past three years."
- Why is your business an excellent investment? Tell prospective buyers why the future is bright for your industry and your business (e.g., long-term contracts, intellectual property, skilled employees, proven processes, revenue and profit growth, etc.).

- How much is the asking price? There are conflicting views here. If you don't cite a price, you risk inquiries from buyers who aren't qualified. However, if you cite a price you risk scaring potential buyers. We suggest you take the risk and tell buyers what you are expecting in terms of revenue and profit multiples.
- The teaser will make bold claims (that's why it's called a *teaser*), but every statement that it contains must be true and verifiable. Don't make hockey stick projections of future revenue unless you can back them up with bottoms-up customer data. Also ensure information in the teaser is not competitively sensitive.

Even with a carefully selected distribution list, more than 90 percent of the people who receive the teaser won't be interested in buying your company even after a follow-up phone discussion from your broker. Responses to Internet postings and ads in trade magazines are even worse—nearly all of those are time-consuming tire kickers. That's why you limit information in the teaser—to avoid sharing facts and figures with people who have no intention of buying your business.

If you retain a business broker, he will maintain confidentially while interviewing all of the respondents to select buyers who are serious and financially qualified. At the conclusion of the screening interviews, you should know:

- Why the buyer wants to purchase your business
- Their experience in your industry
- When they want to close the transaction
- Their financial capacity to finance the purchase
- Their willingness to meet your goals in selling the business

At this point in the process, qualified buyers will be given a numbered copy of the selling memorandum, but only after they execute a Non-Disclosure Agreement. A few days later, the broker will confirm the buyer's continued interest in your business, and arrange for you and the buyer to meet to discuss a deal. If the buyer isn't interested, your broker will request that he either return the selling memorandum or certify in writing that it was destroyed. You don't want the selling memorandum floating around and possibly falling into a competitor's hands.

MISTAKE #27

MAKING A BAD FIRST IMPRESSION

Finding a buyer is a lot like hooking a fish on the line—you only get one chance to reel it into the boat.

The founder of a start-up web company had a fifteen-minute opportunity to present his business to the angel investment group where Dick is a member. Relative to describing his product and market, the founder's pitch was thorough and well-rehearsed. The content was insightful, the viewgraphs were professional, and he spoke with passion and authority.

However, just two minutes into the presentation he lost the group's attention because the material was directed toward technologists rather than investors. He failed to address the predictable concerns of men and women who might invest millions of dollars in his company. After the pitch, the group discussed the opportunity briefly, decided they weren't interested, and moved on to the next investment candidate.

Unfortunately, similar misguided presentations are given frequently by owners who are selling their business. Too often a prospective buyer is the first to hear the pitch because the seller didn't bother to practice it in front of people who would provide constructive feedback. At the end of such presentations, buyers usually say, *"I'll think about it and get back to you"*—but the end result is buyers walk away from the deal and sellers are left wondering why.

When he offered his company for sale, Dick was lucky to work with a broker who insisted on rehearsed presentations and scripted meetings with buyers. The process began by identifying and prioritizing over forty potential acquirers who were both financially qualified and interested in companies like Dick's. Half were eliminated for various reasons, and a teaser was sent to twenty-one companies. Dick also prepared a written management presentation that served as the selling memorandum. While the broker contacted buyers who received the teaser to gage their interest, he also worked with Dick and his managers to rehearse the presentation.

The first step in developing a selling memorandum is deciding what information to give potential buyers. Obviously, buyers can't make an investment decision without basic information. On the other hand, if the buyer is a competitor or supplier, providing too much information could be damaging. The question is: "*Can this information be used to compete against my company?*" If the answer is *yes*, leave the information out of the document. Highly confidential information can be shown during due diligence to a buyer who is willing to meet your price and goals.

Ensure that each potential buyer signs a Non-Disclosure Agreement (NDA) before receiving the selling memorandum. Some people doubt the enforceability of an NDA but, practically speaking, it is a goodwill gesture that usually eliminates anyone who isn't a serious buyer. To help enforce the NDA, number each copy of your selling memorandum and repeat the number with a copyright notice on each page in the document. Also put a bolded note on the cover page to state that this document was given to the reader subject to terms and conditions of an NDA, and that the NDA will be enforced to the full extent of the law.

A selling memorandum is both a business offering and a marketing brochure. It answers many questions buyers have about your company, and explains why it is a good investment. In one document, the selling memorandum describes your company's history and growth; products, services, and customers; current and projected financial performance; management team; and operations. It also projects the cash flow it will generate for a new owner, specifies your asking price, and explains why you are selling. In addition, specify whether you want to work with the company after the sale, or just walk away. If you intend to stay with the company, define your potential post-closing role. The purpose of the selling memorandum is to encourage a buyer to take the next step—but it doesn't attempt to answer every question a buyer might have.

The selling memorandum provides facts, but it is more than just a facts-and-figures document. It must provide information that stimulates interest and a market summary that helps buyers see the strengths and potential of your business. It focuses on the upside of your business, of course, but it can't ignore weaknesses. Major issues must be addressed in terms of planned response. The selling memorandum presents facts about your business in a favorable way, but everything must be true and verifiable. You can be sure the buyer will verify the data and projections in due diligence, and require you to warrant the information's accuracy in the Purchase & Sale Agreement.

In Dick's case, five buyers asked for the selling memorandum as an oral presentation, and three others received it in hard copy. In each case, the document was customized to the buyer's specific interests. Prior to delivering an oral presentation to buyers, Dick, the President, and Vice President delivered a dry run to the broker and his staff. Dick recapped the company's history and explained why he was selling. The President addressed financial performance, service offerings, operating strategies, customer base, and staff credentials. The Vice President presented the sales projections, and gave an overview of the business development program and methodology. The dry runs were hugely valuable in terms of increasing the chances of a sale. The broker and his staff didn't pull any punches; they asked probing questions and provided insightful criticisms that sharpened the message and polished the delivery.

When presenting your business to a potential buyer, focus on the three main questions he wants you to answer:

(1) *Why are you selling?* Buyers wonder why you would sell a very successful business. Provide a sincere answer that explains why this is the right time for you to sell and reduce the buyer's unspoken fear that you are scrambling to abandon a sinking ship.

(2) *How bright is the future?* Provide projections for future revenue, profit, and cash flow; substantiate them by describing the basis for the projections and citing how accurately you were able to project your company's recent results.

(3) *What are the hidden opportunities and risks?* Address things that might develop that are not explicitly included in your quantitative projections, including opportunities that are unique to the buyer. Be honest in acknowledging challenges and describing actions you have taken or recommend to reduce risk. Buyers like to see an upside since they want to pay a little less than the business is really worth.

Obviously, you must answer the first question personally. But if your management team is important for the sale, let them address the second and third questions. After all, they are the ones who will help the buyer realize the projections, capitalize on opportunities, and avoid risks. In addition, the management team should be prepared to tell the buyer why they are not buying the business.

When you finish the presentation, answer the buyer's questions with explanations that showcase the business's strengths. For example, if the buyer asks about your operations staff, answer the question by explaining how you find, hire, and retain (e.g., employment agreements and incentive programs) employees; how you train them to maximize productivity; and how you manage salaries and benefits. Remember, though, that everything you say must be verifiable during due diligence.

Buyers usually start with quantitative questions, and then move on to more probing strategic questions. Answer those questions honestly too, even though your tendency will be to avoid them. Describe any market or economic issues you face, and identify the challenges you see. It is crucial to disclose any business or legal issues that you know about so they don't become deal-killing surprises in due diligence.

However, if the buyer requests competitive information like your marketing plan or procedures manual, respond that those materials will be provided during due diligence. Do not share your company's "secret sauce," client contact information, or detailed financial information until the buyer submits a written offer in a LOI and you accept the offer. In addition, don't let the buyer contact customers or employees who aren't involved in the sale, since a rumor that the company is for sale could hurt the business. Also, let your broker handle questions about asking price, payment structure, or terms and conditions. Explain that when the buyer submits a written offer, you will involve your attorney, CPA, and broker in the negotiations as required to make the deal work. Emphasize that you intend the transaction to be a win-win for the buyer, yourself, your employees, and your customers. The measure of success for your presentation is that it deepens the buyer's interest and makes a good first impression. You only get one chance to make a good first impression!

MISTAKE #28

LACK OF INTELLIGENCE ABOUT A BUYER

When meeting a buyer, you must know your own position, of course. But it's equally important for you to know their position and to anticipate how they will react to yours.

During the seven months required to sell his company, Dick worked with his broker essentially every day. One afternoon after rehearsing the management presentation for hours, the broker and Dick's management team went to a restaurant to review the next steps over nachos and beer. Several important questions arose about the buyer's actions in previous acquisitions. The broker took out his Blackberry, made a few inquiries, and in short order had the answers. Today's high-speed communications tools enabled us to research the buyer's motivations and acquisition style, and incorporate that knowledge into our strategy. That particular deal didn't go through, but the information put us in a better position to prepare for the transaction that eventually closed.

Useful information about potential buyers is available from multiple sources. All publicly-traded corporations must file quarterly (10-Q) and annual reports (10-K) with the Securities and Exchange Commission (SEC). Those reports, which are available online for public viewing, usually provide significant insights into the buyer's financial condition, expansion goals, previous acquisitions, and ownership structure. Such information will tell you why they are planning to expand, and in what geographic areas and product/service lines. Google searches of the company name, their product names, and their officers' names usually yield strategically valuable information. Of course, Dunn & Bradstreet reports, the company's website, and searchable newspaper databases are also a gold mine of helpful information.

What is the buyer trying to accomplish in purchasing your company? If you can't answer that question with specifics, do more research. Is the buyer under pressure to increase its revenue and profitability? Since organic growth is slow in many industries, publicly-traded companies must buy businesses because winning new clients and developing new products from the ground up takes too long. If that is the case, highlight the growth aspects of your company and your market in meetings with the buyer. On the other hand, the buyer may be looking to expand into a specific new industry, area, or customer base. For example, strategic buyers are looking for branded offerings in health care, cyber-security, the environment, and energy. If that is the case, highlight your unique product and service offerings in those fields.

One way to find out what a buyer is looking for is to ask him—and your broker is in a great position to do exactly that. Many sellers are not able to see their company through the eyes of the buyer, so they need an experienced negotiator to showcase the relevant value of their business. After you accept an offer, your company will be off the market, so the pre-offer period is the best time to ask about the buyer's attraction to your company. Since he will handle initial buyer inquiries, your broker is in the perfect position to ask questions like:

- Have you purchased businesses in the past? Which ones?
- What were the sources of funds for those transactions?
- When would you like to close a deal? Why that particular date?
- What are your sources of funds for the transaction? Is financing in place, and what security have you offered for the financing?
- What are the criteria for your purchase decision?
- Are there any deal-breakers?
- What other companies are you considering?

These questions help determine a buyer's M&A expertise, the urgency of closing a transaction, and issues with financial capacity. The last two questions usually stimulate a fruitful conversation about what the buyer is seeking in your business, and whether the buyer is considering other businesses in other price ranges. Brokers are shrewd in asking questions. When a buyer responds, they don't interrupt. Instead they let the buyer talk and talk—even ramble. It's amazing how many sensitive details a buyer will reveal during off-the-cuff responses, especially when they are uncomfortable with the answer they need to give.

Brokers also are able to differentiate between hot prospects and tire kickers, and deal with always-sensitive inquiries from competitors. Hot prospects have:

- Specific reasons for wanting to buy a business like yours
- The ability to run your business effectively
- Realistic pricing expectations
- The financial capability to buy your company

Tire kickers, on the other hand, can't or aren't willing to discuss their buying goals, management capabilities, or financial resources. Their answers confirm that they do not really know what they want or when they want to close.

Purchase inquiries from competitors may or may not be legitimate, so they are always risky. A competitor may genuinely be interested in buying your company as a strategic acquisition. Or a key manager from a competing company may be ready and able to venture out and run his own company. But in both cases, the prospect could be more devious or curious than serious. A competitor who is fishing for information about your company generally will be reluctant to share sensitive information about his business and will refuse to sign a Non-Disclosure Agreement. Experienced brokers are astute in differentiating real buyers from cold prospects and devious competitors.

Understanding your buyer's motives and speaking his language will make the transaction go smoother at a minimum, and sometimes it can increase the closing price. In any case, you are in a stronger bargaining position if you can describe your company's value in terms that a buyer understands. By identifying realistic opportunities to expand the buyer's revenue base, being accretive to his earnings, and improving the ratios he uses to measure performance and make decisions, you will set your business above competing candidates. When you understand the buyer's motivations and limitations, you are a more effective negotiator and you increase the chances of closing the deal.

MISTAKE #29

ONE BUYER IS NO BUYER

Without competition, the buyer has no sense of urgency. He controls the deal flow, leaving you with little bargaining power.

A business owner hired a broker and put his company on the market. The business had a record of consistent growth and profitability, and a set of loyal customers that was attractive to multiple buyers. The broker prepared a stimulating teaser, distributed it to thirty-five potential buyers and planned to hold a limited competition. The first offer was received in a written Letter of Intent (LOI) five days after the teaser was issued.

The seller was ecstatic! The LOI offered 90 percent of the asking price—higher than he expected. What's more, a potential liability that concerned the seller was acknowledged in the LOI and, therefore, was included in the offer price. As expected, the LOI required the seller to indemnify the buyer against that liability in the sale agreement. The exclusivity clause specified ten days to confirm the company's overall performance, and ninety days to develop the sale agreement.

The broker's advice was to wait until other offers were received. But the seller, anxious to close the deal, signed the LOI. At the end of the ten-day period, the buyer confirmed the offer price in writing as required by the LOI. The deal seemed to be flowing smoothly until the unusual liability caused due diligence to drag on. The exclusionary period was extended to 120 days by mutual agreement. A week prior to the end of the 120-day period, however, the buyer withdrew without explanation.

The passage of time is the enemy of all deals. The seller offered a price reduction to resurrect the deal, but the buyer had lost interest for some reason. The seller had absorbed enormous transaction costs, not to mention the emotional trauma. Fortunately, he was able to keep the transaction confidential relative to middle managers and employees. It took eighteen months for the company to regain the momentum it lost during the aborted four-month negotiation period.

Dick had a similar experience in selling his company—but with a better outcome. A month after distributing the teaser and providing presentations, a LOI was received from a buyer. Price, terms, and post-closing roles were negotiated and the LOI was ready to sign. But the buyer knew he was the only bidder and delayed signing for three weeks while he decided how to merge a consulting practice into his technology business. An equity investor, knowing that an LOI was close to being signed, submitted an LOI with better terms and won the deal. The LOI was signed in four days, and the deal closed six months later.

Serious buyers know the price they are willing to pay for a company that fits their criteria. They are looking for a business priced in a narrow range. Based on information in a teaser, buyers can quickly decide if an interesting business is worth further consideration. An asking price that seems too high is a deal-killer; the buyer simply moves on to the next deal without a second thought. If your business is priced in the range, however, it gets a thorough look and the buyer may submit a draft LOI. When a savvy buyer knows he is the only bidder, he offers a price at the bottom of the acceptable price range and hopes you will accept it. That's why accepting the first offer you receive may be a costly mistake. One buyer is like no buyer. Without competition, the buyer has no urgency to close the deal until they extract concessions. The seller, having little leverage except to walk away from the deal, is in a weak position.

Most LOIs contain an exclusionary period that restricts a seller from marketing his business for thirty days (or longer). During that period, the buyer conducts due diligence and the Purchase & Sale Agreement is negotiated. However, if a buyer knows other LOIs were submitted, the seller is in position to push the buyer for concessions. An alternative is to ask the buyer to pay the seller's transaction costs as a breakup fee if the buyer walks away for other than specified reasons. However, this somewhat risky provision may cause the buyer to walk, and the buyer still may be able to structure a walk-away without paying the breakup fee. Having other buyers waiting at the end of the exclusionary period can be worth as much as 10 percent in the price and produce more favorable terms. Be patient and wait for at least a second buyer!

MISTAKE #30

RELYING ON A HANDSHAKE

Your leverage shrinks when you sign the Letter of Intent,
so get the structure of the deal, the selling price, the payment
terms, and other essential terms and conditions all in writing!

A client approached his attorney with a signed LOI negotiated with the buyer and was jubilant about the sale price. Excitedly, he said, "*The buyer and I are tight. We understand each other; we shook hands. This will be the fastest deal you've ever done.*" The lawyer congratulated him and commented that, other than the price, it was the most one-sided LOI he'd ever seen: just a page long, a ninety-day exclusionary period, and only a few vague terms and conditions, among other seller-leaning features. To no one's surprise, the first draft of the Purchase & Sale Agreement left a lot to be negotiated. It set the liability cap at 100 percent of the sales price, retained 35 percent of the proceeds in escrow, and gave the buyer a five-year recovery period.

The transaction eventually closed, but it took eight months to undo the one-sided LOI, and negotiate reasonable terms and conditions in the sale agreement. Frustrations were intense on both sides of the table, and transaction costs were astronomical. Normally, the seller wants as much detail as possible in the LOI and a short exclusionary period. However, the buyer would prefer to wait until after due diligence to lock in terms and conditions, and wants the seller off the market as long as possible. The seller has maximum leverage over the buyer just prior to signing the LOI—especially when there are multiple bidders. Immediately after the LOI is signed, negotiating leverage shifts to the buyer.

Before you can sell your business, you will receive an offer, respond with a counteroffer, negotiate terms and conditions, and sign an LOI. The offer generally starts at first in verbal form, but soon becomes a LOI that documents the buyer's proposed price and terms. It is an exciting but stressful day when you begin negotiating an LOI with an external or internal buyer who is really interested in buying your company. Signing the LOI signals the start of due diligence where the buyer confirms the condition of your business and examines its finances and operations; and you confirm the buyer's management and financial wherewithal to complete the deal. Everyone optimistically looks forward to the day (often six or more months in the future) when negotiations will be finished, both parties will sign the sale agreement, and the payments and escrows will be transferred.

Buyers often get nervous when they put an offer in writing. They will examine and re-examine everything from the sales price, to what it takes to manage your company, to what will happen if the deal falls apart. For the most part, your broker will assuage the buyer's fears and encourage him to submit an acceptable offer. The buyer knows, of course, that an LOI is not binding on either party—but it doesn't feel that way! Most LOIs include contingencies—conditions to be met before the offer will become legally binding or the buyer's deposit could be forfeited. For example, buyers typically make their offer contingent on due diligence results and securing financing for the deal.

When preparing to submit an LOI, the buyer often will ask for more information than you're willing to provide at that time. If the buyer asks for confidential information, tell him that you will have the information available for his review during due diligence, which will begin after the LOI is signed. If he insists, invite him to specify each of his requests in the LOI. It's better to sign an LOI with multiple conditions than not to sign one at all.

The LOI will determine how the deal will be structured; and how much, when, and in what form you will be paid. Deals that pay all cash at closing are unusual. Therefore, your personal financial and income tax planning must be done before you start to negotiate an LOI, and you should determine if you are willing to continue with the company after the acquisition and if so, for how long. Your financial planning provides criteria for negotiating price and payment terms.

In addition, you must decide whether or not you can afford to give seller financing, and the terms and security you are willing to accept in return for such financing. For example, if the buyer is using third-party financing, any seller financing generally will be subordinate to the third-party debt. Furthermore, some types of financing (e.g., SBA loans) place additional conditions on seller financing.

The transaction may involve accepting stock in the buyer's company in lieu of cash. Be careful: If the stock has a market value and you are restricted from selling it for a period, then you could face a significant tax liability and not have the cash to pay it. Part of the proceeds may be retained in escrow accounts for six months or longer. Again you must understand the tax consequences of the escrows or you might have to face an ugly surprise on April 15th!

Income and estate tax planning is critical prior to executing the LOI. For example, months before the LOI was signed, Dick transferred most of his stock to a family trust in exchange for a second-to-die annuity for his wife and himself. Stuart helped form the trust, served as trustee, and signed the LOI and sale agreement in that capacity. Intricate financial planning like that would have been difficult to complete after the LOI was signed, which could have jeopardized the deal.

The LOI will contain a broad range of other terms and conditions that are important to the deal. As the seller, your preference should be to have more detail, rather than less, in the LOI. The clauses that could be inserted in an LOI are too many to discuss here in entirety, but a few of the controversial and common ones are:

- *Structure of the Deal.* The LOI should state whether the acquisition is a stock or an asset sale. There is often tension between the seller and buyer on this issue because the income tax consequences and risks differ for the buyer and seller in each structure.
- *Extent and Timing of Due Diligence.* Some LOIs will specify the date by which the seller must provide information to a third-party lender. Failure to provide the information on a timely basis may extend the due diligence or the financing contingency periods.
- *Continuing Role.* The LOI should state that you will, or will not, remain with the business after closing. If you do plan to stay, the clause should specify for how long, in what role, whether you will be an employee or consultant, and with what pay and benefits.
- *Exclusionary Period.* Keep it short—thirty days is about right unless the business involves unusual real estate or contractual requirements, or environmental impacts. Don't be in a rush to close since the buyer can use that against you.

- *Escrows.* Don't let a buyer get away by saying the sales agreement will "contain the customary escrows." If possible, require the LOI to specify what escrows, how long the money will be retained, and how the amount of the escrow will be determined. Furthermore, if the escrows will be interest-bearing, ensure that you have the right to receive a quarterly payment from the escrows sufficient to pay the income taxes due on the interest earned.

- *Price Reduction by Buyer.* Include a clause saying that, if the buyer reduces the price, the seller (you) have the option to end the exclusionary period immediately. Depending on the quality of your financial statements, it may be better to state the purchase price in terms of a formula to prevent the deal from collapsing if a surprise shows up in due diligence.

- *Agreement Not-to-Compete.* The buyer will probably insist that you sign a covenant not-to-compete with your former company, and not to approach its customers or solicit its employees. The LOI should specify a reasonable time period and geographic area for the not-to-compete agreement.

- *Restrictions on Operations.* The buyer will want to restrict your investments and other major transactions during the due diligence period. Ensure the restrictions are reasonable and don't conflict with actions that you already plan to take.

- *Retention of Key Employees and Clients.* The buyer may condition closing on the retention of key employees and/or key clients. In some cases, the buyer also may require a certain structure in the purchase agreement to avoid termination of contracts and to be able to claim your performance history.

If the draft LOI doesn't contain all of the terms and conditions you feel are necessary, have your attorney prepare additional clauses and submit them to the buyer to be inserted into the draft LOI that he originated.

Before signing the LOI, which takes your company off the market during the exclusionary period, do due diligence on the buyer's financial capabilities to complete the transaction. In normal times, some deals fail to close after the LOI is signed because the buyer can't pay the purchase price. When the economy is in a tailspin and lending standards are tight, the number of deals that fail to close for lack of buyer financing increases. In many cases, a seller will be better advised to accept a slightly lower purchase price from a financially capable buyer than to accept a higher price from a buyer who is on the edge financially. Reasonable due diligence prior to signing the LOI will save you time and money in the long run by avoiding traumas and transaction costs on a deal that never closes.

Signing the LOI is like dropping the puck to begin a hockey game—it signifies the start of the action and the fights. So before you think about signing an LOI, review it thoroughly and have your attorney, broker, and CPA evaluate it too. If you are like most sellers, your deal-or-no-deal decision will focus on the proposed price. That can be a costly mistake! What the buyer is actually buying (i.e., stock or assets), how and when you will be paid, and how the price is allocated to various asset classes will determine how much after-tax cash you actually take away from the deal because they affect your tax liabilities. In these areas, the advice of your CPA and attorney is as a good as gold—literally worth money in the bank.

MISTAKE #31

RIGID PRICE EXPECTATIONS

When is enough enough? Be open to accepting the offer most likely to close instead of the highest bid.

D uring the peak of the Iraqi War, a logistics services company's annual revenue skyrocketed from $10 million to $68 million, and its pre-tax profits soared from $1 million to $14 million. The company's rapid growth and high profits attracted a broad range of bidders to the limited auction. Eventually, the competition narrowed to just two bidders: one with extensive experience in the seller's industry, and the other whose strategic objective was to gain a foothold in military logistics where it had limited experience and only a small share of the market. Both bidders were very concerned that the seller's 20 percent profit rate might be unsustainable.

The inexperienced buyer won the auction with an offer of 1.5 times revenue and all-cash at closing—$2 million higher than the experienced buyer was willing to bid. The seller popped the champagne corks and celebrated when the LOI was signed and due diligence began. But the negotiations were cluttered with issues because the successful bidder didn't understand government contracts, and was spooked by relatively common clauses. For example, the buyer was concerned that the "most-favored customer" clause in government contracts would reduce profits on their bread-and-butter commercial contracts.

After two gruesome months of due diligence, the buyer walked away. The seller picked the wrong buyer because of a price differential under 2 percent. Two years later, the company's revenue and profit were flat and it sold to another buyer for just one times the revenue—$30 million less than the experienced (but rejected) buyer offered only two years earlier. When is enough enough? When a seller receives multiple offers with acceptable prices, is it worth the risk to take the highest bidder, or would a more effective strategy be to accept the offer of the bidder most likely to close?

The LOI sets a sale price for your business, but that number and the payment terms are likely to change as due diligence proceeds and your business operates in a world of change, which is why using a formula in the LOI to set the price is a good idea. The sale price goes down more often than it goes up before the deal closes. Changes that could affect the final sale price include:

- *Asset or Stock Sale.* Buyers frequently are willing to pay more in an asset sale than in an equivalent stock sale because an asset sale has lower risks and provides substantial income tax benefits to the buyer. However, an asset sale often has adverse tax consequences to the seller.

- *Excluded Items.* You can respond to a buyer's request to reduce the price by excluding specific items from the sale (e.g., receivables, real estate, and equipment). Real estate and equipment that are essential to the business can be leased to the buyer, and receivables can be converted into cash that you keep.

- *Payment Terms.* Generally, the more cash you want at closing, the more pressure the buyer will apply to lower the price. If you accept escrows, earn-outs, deferred payments, or offer seller financing, the buyer has less leverage. Deferred payments and earn-out payments can be structured to give you favorable capital gains treatment.

- *Actual Condition of Your Business.* If the buyer determines during due diligence that your business, contracts, customer base, staff, or equipment are less valuable than you claimed, he will want to reduce the price.

- *Tax Consequences.* Buyers will agree to a higher price if they can allocate it in a way that produces short-term tax write-offs such as depreciating equipment or compensating you as an employee or a consultant. Similarly, as the seller, you can accept a lower price if it is taxed as capital gains rather than as ordinary income.

Be creative and flexible in negotiating the Purchase & Sale Agreement—an area where M&A-experienced attorneys and CPAs will earn every penny of their fees. For example, if the buyer wants to provide less cash at closing and you have confidence in his management ability and credit, offset the request with new earn-outs and/or higher fees for your post-closing services. By restructuring the deal, you may be able to accept a lower price than the one cited in the LOI and close the deal with the same (sometimes more) after-tax proceeds.

Representations and warranties, an essential part of every Purchase & Sale Agreement, also can affect the amount you realize from the sale. The sale agreement contains representations and warranties for both the seller and buyer, but there are usually many more on the seller's side than on the buyer's side. In agreeing to representations and warranties, you are telling the buyer: *"Everything that I have told you about my company is accurate to the best of my knowledge, and I haven't left out any liabilities or material facts that could affect its future."*

For example, warranties include declarations that:

- Financial statements accurately present the company's condition.
- You have legal authority to approve the sale.
- You have clear title to the assets you are selling.
- You know of no liabilities beyond those identified in financial statements and other schedules.
- You know of no legal actions that may be taken against the company other than those explicitly identified in the agreement.
- You have filed all tax returns, paid all taxes, and are not subject to government audits.

Just to cite a few. Extensive additional representations would apply to companies that do business with the U.S. government. Be certain you honestly can make such statements because, if the buyer can prove you omitted or misrepresented material facts, he may be able to recover money from escrows, avoid repaying the seller loan, withhold earn-out payments, or sue you. During negotiations, tell the truth about your company's finances, assets, government audits, taxes, lawsuits, and other liabilities.

The Purchase & Sale Agreement also will specify certain rights and obligations of the seller and the buyer. For example, the buyer has the right to reduce the price for post-closing variances in asset values (e.g., receivables and inventory) and liabilities. If possible, spell out how any reductions will be calculated to avoid costly and prolonged post-closing disputes. Such amounts may be taken from escrow accounts established for that purpose. The buyer also has obligations to you, especially if you continue as an employee or a consultant, are entitled to earn-outs, or are providing seller financing. The Purchase & Sale Agreement should also specify quantitative limitations on the buyer's ability to recover amounts from you in excess of the escrows. The buyer's obligations to you often will require the buyer to provide access to the company's financial records, carry insurance, and maintain a minimum working capital level until the purchase price is paid in full.

The bottom line is: *be flexible about price.* During development of the Purchase & Sale Agreement, you and the buyer will make countless trade-offs and concessions. Stuart tells his clients: "*The sign of a successful negotiation is that both sides walk away from the table feeling some pain.*" Obviously, you will protect your interests, but you are treading on thin ice if you try to increase your net proceeds from the value in the LOI. If you feel that you deserve more for the business, put an earn-out provision into the payment structure so you can benefit from future performance and still be gentle on the buyer with respect to cash at closing. Remember: your objective is to close a deal that works rather than to extract every possible nickel from the buyer.

MISTAKE #32

SLEEPING THROUGH DUE DILIGENCE

As the seller, you have dual purposes in due diligence. First to actively ensure the buyer is able to purchase and manage your company; and second, to help the buyer research your company.

In 1994, Dick had a dreadful experience in an early attempt to sell his company when it was relatively small. Whirlwind discussions with the buyer produced an LOI just three weeks after the first meeting. There seemed to be exceptional synergy between Dick's government projects and the buyer's work with commercial firms and government agencies. After consulting with his attorney during the negotiations, Dick signed the LOI and due diligence began.

Dick viewed due diligence as solely an exercise for the buyer, and directed his managers to help the buyer research company records and analyze its operations. The LOI specified that Dick would remain with the company as Vice President, and half of the selling price was scheduled to be paid as earnouts. Negotiating the Purchase & Sale Agreement wasn't easy, but Dick and the buyer finally agreed to terms. However, the buyer failed to bring a check to the closing table as specified in the agreement. He planned to use cash from Dick's accounts to make the payment due at closing. Apparently the buyer was having severe cash flow problems, which Dick didn't know because he hadn't done any seller due diligence.

Dick and his attorney left the closing table and took a walk through a nearby park to discuss the situation. The attorney advised Dick not to sign the sale agreement—he took the advice. Dick didn't know it then, but he dodged a bullet that day because a year later, the buyer declared bankruptcy. The failed acquisition was a very expensive lesson in lack of due diligence by the seller. Transaction costs on Dick's side alone exceeded $20 thousand exclusive of operational disruptions!

Due diligence, which is performed after the LOI is signed, can make or break a deal from either the buyer's or the seller's side. LOIs usually are contingent on the buyer's investigation of the seller's business, but your LOI also should be contingent on your evaluation of the buyer. If you think of yourself as a detective, then you will love due diligence. As the seller, you must do more than just cooperate with the buyer's due diligence team; you must do your own review of the buyer's financial wherewithal and ability to run your business.

Due diligence usually can be completed in 30–60 days, unless the sale is complicated by government contracts, environmental issues, real estate ownership, outstanding legal proceedings or issues, or other unusual circumstances. The buyer's purpose in due diligence is to ensure your company meets the expectations you created during earlier meetings and in the selling memorandum. The buyer's investigation will include your assets and liabilities, revenue and profits, operations, human resource matters, contracts, legal issues, and other matters unique to your industry and company. The LOI should include a clause to ensure information obtained by the buyer during due diligence is not disclosed to anyone other than the buyer's CPA and attorney. If for any reason your business is not like you said it would be, the buyer may renegotiate the selling price, insert additional conditions and contingencies in the sale agreement, or walk away.

It is in your best interest to help the buyer finish his investigation as quickly as possible. So respond promptly to every buyer request because delays don't just extend the transaction, they kill deals. In addition, the LOI may provide that the financing contingency period begins only *after* you provide the financial information required by the buyer's financing source. In that case, getting the information to his lender should receive your top attention.

Some sellers assemble documents in their CPA's office for the buyer to review. We recommend that you give the buyer access to your CPA and attorney to answer any questions about your business. Unless your attorney advises otherwise in a specific situation, information about your company should be provided for review only. It should not be reproduced and given to the buyer.

To expedite due diligence, don't wait until the last minute to locate documents or compile data. If possible, your CPA should have your most recent tax returns and current financial information prepared and ready to give to the buyer right after the LOI is signed. Download a due diligence checklist online for a nominal price (or get one for free from your CPA or attorney) and gather information on the checklist even as you are looking for a buyer. Virtual online due diligence review tools also are available in today's all-digital world if such techniques are appropriate in your industry. Not only will such early planning avoid chaotic last-minute projects, but it will keep the deal moving once the LOI is signed.

While you shouldn't showcase adverse information, don't conceal it either. If your business has issues, the buyer probably will find them in due diligence. When a buyer finds problems that you have not told him about, his first reaction is likely to be: *"What else is there that I haven't found yet?"* and his second reaction will be to ask for an increase in the escrows required under the LOI. Even if a problem escapes detection, it is highly likely to be found after closing when the buyer could withhold payments on grounds that you misrepresented the business. Since the Purchase & Sale Agreement will contain representations and warranties, honesty is more than just a good policy—it's a necessity. So if your business faces problems, reveal them to the buyer early in the process and share your strategy for correcting the problems or mitigating their impact.

As the seller, you also have several crucial due diligence tasks to do yourself. First, since most LOIs make the deal contingent on the buyer being able to secure financing, if you have not done so prior to signing the LOI, then evaluate the buyer's financial wherewithal during due diligence. Second, you must determine the buyer's future plans for your business to ensure he can manage the business after the deal closes. If you intend to provide seller financing, your most important decision may be: *Can the buyer run the business well enough to pay me?* While the buyer is investigating your business, you must determine if he has any adverse limitations in financial condition or management ability. In other words, do your own due diligence!

The warning flags that extensive due diligence by the seller will be required begin to wave when the LOI specifies seller financing, deferred payments, earn-outs, or a continuing role for you in the business:

- *Seller Financing.* If you will accept deferred payments or provide seller financing, confirm the buyer's creditworthiness and ability to run the business to produce the cash flow required to pay you and any third-party lenders, since your loan will be subordinate to these lenders.

- *Earn-outs.* If you agree to earn-outs that depend on the business's success, confirm the buyer's plan for operating the business. Also ensure the formula for earn-out payments is clearly specified and that you have the right to examine financial information related to the earn-outs. As President Reagan said: *"Trust but verify!"*

- *Continuing Role.* If you will stay with the business in a full-time role, confirm that you can tolerate the buyer's decision-making style and personal reputation for the duration of your involvement. Also, the sale agreement should specify your duties, performance measures, goals, and authority in order to prevent either side from becoming frustrated with the post-closing relationship.

Be especially cautious when the buyer has plans that endanger your key customer and supplier relationships, employee retention, or the company's cash flow. If the buyer refuses to abandon such plans, revise the payment structure so you are paid in full at closing, and limit your ongoing role to short time. The goal of seller due diligence is to ensure that you receive the full value for the business that you are selling.

MISTAKE #33

SHOWING YOUR WARTS

It's much less expensive to remove financial warts before your company goes on the market than to have the buyer discover them during due diligence.

A CEO was delighted and surprised when the manufacturer of the equipment he distributed offered to buy part of his business. The offer was out of the blue and in his words: *"Last year was our best year ever, and I didn't have time to pretty things up for a buyer."* But after hiring a CVE to verify the value of his company and consulting with his lawyer, he accepted their generous offer.

What should have been a routine transaction took thirteen months to close. Inaccurate accounts receivable, accounts payable, and inventory records were issues in the asset sale. He hadn't performed annual audits, and the buyer insisted that one be done before closing. After the audit, the price was reduced because his working capital was less than industry average and a substantial portion of the remaining price became earn-outs in the Asset Purchase Agreement. After celebrating the closing, the CEO lamented: *"I had no idea how complex and frustrating financial negotiations could be. I would have gotten a boatload more money if I had gotten professional help years ago."*

A second CEO operated a lucrative business in a building that he owned. Unfortunately, a family matter forced him to sell the company and move out of the area. He found a buyer, but the bank wouldn't grant a loan big enough to purchase the business and the building. The deal was salvaged through an asset sale. The CEO continued to own the building, and leased it to the new owner. However, the transaction had unfavorable tax consequences to the seller. The lesson learned is never put real estate into an operating company—better to put it in a holding company with a lease-back agreement that maximizes your selling options and provides flexibility in tax planning.

A third CEO could only sell her business to a publicly-traded firm as an asset sale because of liabilities and personal debt on the company's books. For many years, her attorney and CPA had advised her to switch to an S-corporation, but she ignored the advice and her company was still a C-corporation when it was sold. She was able to purchase Errors & Omissions (E&O) insurance against the liabilities. However, when proceeds of the sale were received in the shell company, they were taxed twice: first at the corporate rate and again as ordinary income when she got the cash. Had she converted to an S-corporation, the proceeds would have been taxed only once at the more favorable capital gains tax rate.

A fourth CEO offered his government services company for sale via a broker. A prospective buyer was selected using a limited auction. The business had a record of consistent growth and above-market profits, a portfolio of multi-year contracts, and a highly qualified technical staff. But it also had a huge wart that wasn't revealed before signing the LOI: an unquantifiable, off-balance sheet liability caused by overbillings on government contracts. When the buyer found the issue in due diligence, he withdrew from the transaction.

A fifth company had the practice of recording a sale and creating an account receivable when a client submitted a purchase order. However, the actual price was usually discounted heavily when the merchandise was delivered, and the company used an allowance for bad debt to reconcile the difference. When the company went on the market, buyers and banks walked away because of high bad debt expenses. By changing their accounting practices to recognize an account receivable when the purchase price was fixed, the company's gross income was reduced, but net income remained the same and the bad debts disappeared. Two years later, the company was sold with a much improved balance sheet.

The common thread in these five mistakes is that once your business is on the market, financial warts can be very expensive in terms of price reductions, higher taxes, increased escrows, extended payments, higher legal fees, and inability of the buyer to secure financing at a reasonable interest rate. Financial warts kill more deals than any other single factor. And even when the deal goes through, the negotiations take longer and the deal usually closes at a lower price than specified in the LOI. That being said, if you can't remove a wart before putting your business up for sale, it is essential that you "open the kimono" and cite the wart in the selling memorandum.

While not warts *per se*, some income tax elections may have adverse consequences in a sale transaction. It's common for small and mid-size businesses to elect S-corporation status to eliminate double taxation on earnings. However, an S-election usually causes the owner to accelerate tax-deductible expenses in the last quarter of the fiscal year to minimize the income tax liability. This type of tax planning can negatively impact the buyer's ability to finance the transaction because banks evaluate a company's net income to determine the ability of the borrower to repay the loan. Therefore, the seller's desire to reduce his current-year income tax liability can make it difficult for a buyer to finance a transaction. Also, an S-Corporation may not be able to take advantage of certain income tax benefits in an ESOP transaction.

A second income tax election that may affect the sale is whether your company is taxed on the cash or accrual basis of accounting. Cash basis accounting usually reduces the current income tax liabilities. However, most large companies are required to be on the accrual basis, and if they buy a company, that company also must be on the accrual basis. In such cases, the buyer will require the seller to bear the income tax liability associated with converting from cash to accrual. Depending on your accounts receivable, accounts payable, and other factors, the tax liability may be substantial. However, the IRS allows companies four years to pay the income taxes associated with the conversion from cash to accrual. Generally, a buyer will require an escrow for payment of those taxes.

In closing, it is not unusual for the buyer's team to discover things about your business during due diligence that you didn't even know. If the buyer finds a significant wart during due diligence that you failed to identify, he may lose trust and spend more time looking deeper for other warts. In extreme cases, he may pull the plug on the deal. Anything that delays the transaction or extends the exclusionary period is an enemy of the seller because it increases the chances of the transaction unraveling.

MISTAKE #34

TAKING YOUR EYE
OFF THE BALL

It is essential that you and your top managers stay
focused on your company's performance during due
diligence; the buyer will be watching like a hawk!

Due diligence and negotiating the Purchase & Sale Agreement were stressful for Dick, as they are for most sellers. The original exclusionary period was sixty days, but it was extended twice during the five months from LOI signing to closing. The company missed its sales projections by 20 percent, revenue growth slowed, and profit dropped from over 10 percent to near zero. The executive team had immersed themselves in the deal and taken their collective eye off directing daily operations.

Dick and the company president spent less time wooing new clients and coaching group managers. The buyer peppered the Vice President of Sales with questions about forecasts and proposals. The controller was buried in endless due diligence requests that caused financial statements and invoices to be late. And the Human Resources Director was busy providing records requested by the buyer, so hiring to fill vacancies was slowed. Furthermore, there were substantial transaction expenses for the broker and attorneys. The buyer lost confidence in the company's sales, revenue, and profitability projections. Four months after the LOI was signed, the buyer used a particularly bad month as an opportunity to attempt to negotiate a lower sale price.

Dick worried about repetitive delays in the negotiations. He knew a business owner who, three weeks after signing a LOI, received a subpoena from a government agency. The business owner offered to indemnify the buyer against the matter, but the publicly-traded company withdrew from the transaction. The tempest-in-a-teapot ended several months later when the government closed the inquiry with no adverse findings. Dick's worst nightmare was that something crazy like that might happen to his company and scuttle the deal.

When due diligence begins, clear your calendar for the cacophony of buyer inquiries, what-if speculations from your management team, and inquisitive probing from employees. Running your business and selling it at the same time probably will devour your evenings and weekends, as well as your workdays. To minimize schedule conflicts, delegate as many of your customer contact and management tasks to your senior staff as possible, and schedule time for oversight. Furthermore, plan on the negotiations to drag on longer than expected—they always do!

One thing you can do today to reduce the impact of due diligence on your company's operations is to begin gathering materials that a buyer will want to see. Dick got a due diligence checklist from his CPA about two years before the transaction, and gradually accumulated documents in notebooks for many items on the list. While the checklist identifies hundreds of documents, roughly half of them are static (e.g., equipment and property leases, company charter, and incorporation documents). You can save yourself countless hours and frustrations by starting this monstrous task early.

The period between LOI signing and closing is precarious; so many things can go wrong and most of them are on the seller's side. The buyer selected your company because it offered rewards that outweighed any risks. He was willing to overlook the risks, especially if you identified them in the selling memorandum. However, if new risks arise during due diligence (or the buyer discovers old risks that you didn't identify), the risk-reward balance shifts. The shift may cause the buyer to reduce the offering price or walk away altogether.

A drop in revenue or profits, a key employee leaving, losing a large customer, an emerging legal issue, a breakthrough by a competitor, or a decline in your industry all represent new risks for the buyer. Some of them are beyond your control, but that's why you want the deal to close as quickly as possible after the LOI is signed. Time is the enemy of the seller, and each extension of the exclusionary period increases chances that the transaction will never close. Keep your eye on the operations ball even as you do everything possible to accelerate the due diligence and negotiations process.

MISTAKE #35

LOOSE LIPS SINK SHIPS

Keeping the LOI a secret for several months is nearly impossible. Even if you choose not to brief employees, be prepared to announce the transaction in case word leaks out.

The President, Vice President, and CFO were the three owners of a company, and the only ones who knew it was being sold. Despite having 200 employees, they were able to conceal the transaction while the teaser was issued and the LOI was negotiated. But a month into due diligence, an invoice from the lawyer was sent accidentally to accounts payable. When the clerk read the invoice, she spilled the beans in the kitchen and the news went viral: "*They're selling the business!*" A week later two mid-level managers left the company, and other managers were contacting headhunters. The leak spooked the buyer and killed the deal.

When you put your company on the market, confide the news to the minimum number of trusted managers. Swear them to secrecy using a Non-Disclosure Agreement, and tell them when the LOI has been signed and when due diligence begins. A confidential announcement to key managers is especially vital if their continued employment is important to the buyer. In this case, reassure them that their compensation and job will be secure under the new owner. In addition, develop procedures to conduct negotiations in secrecy, including safe sites for meetings and due diligence reviews. For example, your attorney's, broker's, or CPA's offices are good choices. To avoid leaks, all invoices for the transaction should be sent directly to the owner or a trusted manager.

Most M&A professionals warn that you can't keep your intention to sell your business close enough to your vest. As illustrated in the above story, care is required in processing invoices and other correspondence from lawyers, brokers, and consultants. Other sources of embarrassing leaks are network administrators who have access to sensitive e-mails and data files, and the receptionist and executive assistants who answer phone calls. Until the sale actually closes and you know the new owner will continue business as usual, don't let word slip to employees except for the few that you bring into your confidence.

Letting news leak before the deal is closed can reduce the value of your company. The risks of telling employees about a sale too early are:

- Employees may tell customers, distributors, suppliers, or your bank about the pending transaction.
- Competing businesses may use news of your sale against you in negotiations with customers, distributors, and suppliers.
- Employees may become anxious about the company's future if the transaction drags on too long and progress is erratic.
- Employees may work against the deal because they don't like the buyer, or are afraid of the changes he might make.

If you tell employees and one of them tells a friend who in turn tells a big customer, bad things can happen. Even if you swear employees to secrecy, you can be sure they'll discuss it among themselves and share the news with their spouses and best friends. Such leaks will jeopardize the assets you are selling (e.g., employees, customers, and distribution channels). For example, customers may be angry that you told others before telling them, and reduce future orders with your company.

Dick had a unique situation relative to announcing that his company was being sold: Nearly 80 percent of employees were shareholders. The buyer insisted that shareholders sign the Purchase & Sales Agreement, so Dick announced the sale about a month into due diligence after all major issues had been resolved. Dick, the President, and the company's attorney were present during the employee briefings. In addition, the President, who remained with the company after the sale, updated employees on status and answered employee questions every two weeks.

Employee briefings are time-consuming, but open communication is essential to assuage their concerns. One challenge is that employees ask questions for which the answers do not yet exist; negotiations with the buyer are still in progress in those areas. In addition, prepare to answer the ever-present *what's-in-it-for-me* questions from employees and to calibrate expectations.

It's better to under-promise and over-deliver. For example, tell employees that transactions often take longer than planned because of emerging issues and there is a real chance that the deal will not close. Brokers and M&A attorneys agree that almost one-fourth of all deals fall apart before a sales agreement is signed.

Near the end of due diligence, a buyer will want to interview at least a few of your employees. Control the interviews to maintain the level of confidentiality, and explain that the buyer wants to meet with employees to recognize and reward performance. The new owner may want to offer bonuses to increase retention during the transition if you haven't already implemented an incentive plan to retain executives and key employees. Your attorney should protect you in the Purchase & Sale Agreement in case employees give erroneous or incomplete information to the buyer. That agreement will warrant that "all facts presented by the seller are accurate to the best of seller's knowledge," but it should define you to be the seller and not your employees.

In some cases, the buyer will ask for meetings with your customers and suppliers. If this happens, try to delay the meetings until the buyer's deposit is irrevocable so he has something to lose and, therefore, will be cautious during the meeting. Brief the buyer on any concerns a customer may have prior to the meeting so the buyer is aware of them. Also, brief customers and suppliers in advance of the meeting to alleviate their concerns about the sale. If possible, arrange to attend the meetings.

Since keeping the sale a secret during a long due diligence is nearly impossible, be prepared to immediately brief employees, customers, and suppliers if news leaks. You and the buyer usually will prepare a joint announcement about the deal to be released after closing. However, we recommend that you prepare the announcement early so it is ready in case of a leak. Despite your best efforts to restrict information about the transaction, news of your sale may hit the internal or public rumor mills earlier than you'd like. It may happen in a panic call from an employee, a question from a concerned customer, or even an inquiry from local news media. If things go as planned, you won't use the announcement until after closing. However, having it ready in case word about the sale leaks puts you in position to minimize the damage and prevent the loose lips from sinking your ship!

MISTAKE #36

COMPLEX EARN-OUTS

Earn-outs are a creative and flexible way to deal with uncertainties in the industry, and to close the price gap between the seller's expectations and the buyer's fears.

A CEO received a lowball purchase offer from an equity group who was doing a roll-up in communications networks. His company, which specialized in government projects, had a twelve-year track record of steady growth and reliable profits. In the fourteen months prior to the offer, however, they had submitted seven competitive proposals on multi-year projects that could more than double annual revenue—but all of the awards had been delayed. Conversely, the buyer was afraid the delays indicated that business from the government sector was leveling out, maybe even shrinking.

The negotiation logjam was broken by establishing a base price with all cash at closing, and specifying an earn-out amount for each proposal the company had submitted. Both parties were elated with the solution: the CEO because he was confident about winning the pending contracts during the two-year earn-out period, and the equity group because it was willing to pay more for new multi-year contracts. The sale closed and the roll-up won three of the seven contracts over the two-year period.

A second CEO had a much different experience with earn-outs. He also sold his IT services firm to a roll-up backed by an equity investor. At the time of the sale, the company had thirty-five employees and $4 million in annual revenue. In the selling memorandum, he projected that revenue from existing and new customers combined would climb 20 percent per year. The company had grown nearly 20 percent in each of the last two years, but the equity firm was concerned that 70 percent of that growth came from one customer. The deal closed with half the price in cash and half in stock in the roll-up, and there was a substantial earn-out based on a combination of revenue growth with existing customers and revenue from new customers.

Since the seller had not developed management infrastructure, after closing his company was merged into the larger organization and he was assigned as the Vice President to direct work for his former customers. Unfortunately, he focused on software production and did not allocate time to pursue sales to new customers. To shorten a long story, revenue from new clients fell well short of projections and his largest customer had a major cutback. He received just the minimum earn-out. The CEO stayed with roll-up for two years until it was sold to a public company. Speaking about the earn-out, he said: "*All things considered, I feel I was treated fairly. The earn-out was too complicated to work, and I just plain didn't make my numbers.*"

Sellers, of course, would like to receive their full asking price as all cash at closing. However, the asking price is frequently based on a rosy projection of future revenue and profits. Not surprisingly, buyers often are skeptical about the seller's projections and they fear the industry's down side. Therefore, they value the company less than the asking price. Earn-outs are a creative way to deal with uncertainties in the industry, and to close the price gap between the seller's expectations and the buyer's fears. The most effective earn-outs are based on specific events or measurable performance parameters.

By including earn-outs in a sale agreement, the seller and buyer agree that part of the price will be decided by how well the business performs after closing. If you are confident that your company will grow rapidly, earn-outs are a great way to participate in the upside. Earn-outs usually are linked to winning a new contract, gaining new customers, increasing revenue, increasing gross margin, or employee retention. The amount of the earn-out is determined by a formula specified in the Purchase & Sale Agreement signed at closing. Earn-outs are typically paid in quarterly, semi-annual, or annual installments for a specified duration. They often have a minimum and/or a maximum payout.

Some earn-outs are based on numbers that could be manipulated by the buyer (e.g., EBITDA). Therefore, the sale agreement should specify how to calculate each earn-out and that the calculation should be "made by an independent CPA acceptable to the parties." If complex earn-outs are included in a sale agreement, they should be accompanied by buyer covenants to: (1) retain key employees, (2) not interfere with operations, (3) maintain specified capabilities, (4) not relocate the work, (5) not do anything that would disqualify a bid, and (6) limit the buyer's personal compensation. On the other hand, if the buyer plans to increase profit by reducing costs, he may try to exclude cost savings from the calculation of EBITDA. In any case, best practice is to keep earn-outs simple to avoid the need for complexities in the sale agreement.

As the seller, consider the following *DOs* and *DON'Ts* with respect to negotiating earn-outs:

- Base earn-outs on specific events or measurable performance like winning a competitive contract, renewing a contract, landing a new customer, retaining key employees, total revenue, revenue from a new product or service, or gross margin.
- Avoid structuring earn-outs based on net profit or EBITDA since the cost structure changes when the new buyer takes over.
- Classify earn-outs as increases in the purchase price to qualify for capital gains. Buyers want to treat earn-outs as bonuses to make them deductible, but then they become ordinary income to you.
- Ensure that earn-outs are also beneficial to the buyer.
- If earn-outs are specified in the sale agreement, remain with the company for the entire earn-out period if possible.
- Except for unusual circumstances, the earn-out period should be two years or less.
- Is the earn-out all-or-nothing, or does it have steps? Is it linear or non-linear (e.g., $X for first increment and less for the second)?
- Don't count on getting any of the earn-outs; you should be happy with the base price even if you never get any earn-out money.
- If the buyer is a foreign company, consider an earn-out escrow.

Be flexible in negotiating earn-outs. As the seller, you know more about what is probable than the buyer, so earn-outs should favor you. In our experience, far more than half of earn-outs are achieved. Remember that earn-outs are always situational and, at the end of the day, getting paid depends on the reputation and character of the buyer.

MISTAKE #37

LOANING YOUR MONEY AWAY

Seller financing is common in small business sales, but don't provide seller financing unless you are sure the buyer can repay the loan.

A father and son had worked together in a family business for ten years. The son's responsibilities had grown to the point where he felt he was ready to manage the company. The father, increasingly frustrated by arguments about running the business, agreed to sell his share and retire. To reduce the purchase price to the son, the father agreed to spin off the company's special-use facility into a holding company, and lease it back to the son. Since the son had no resources of his own, the father agreed to provide a seller-financed loan to enable the transfer of ownership.

Six months after the deal closed, the son expanded the business and purchased a new facility—against his father's advice. Costs to convert the new building into a special-use facility quickly exceeded the budget and ate into profits from the old location. When the economy weakened, income dropped and the son was forced to cease making payments on both the lease and the note. Later, he defaulted on the loan on the new building and vendor payments, and was forced to declare bankruptcy.

The father still owned the original building, but in a soft economy it was nearly impossible to sell. Since the father's loan was subordinated to the son's line-of-credit at the local bank, he recovered nothing at the bankruptcy hearing. Unfortunately, the seller's loan did not contain the typical restrictions that are found in a commercial bank loan. Such restrictions would have required the son to provide monthly financial statements to the father, and would have required the father's written approval for major investments like buying and renovating a building.

Seller financing is common in small business sales, but you should provide a seller-financed loan *only* if you are sure the buyer can repay the loan. If you have lingering concerns about the buyer's capability to make payments, then invest extra time and effort in due diligence and loan documentation. Just because the buyer is a family member does not mean you shouldn't protect yourself as if he was a stranger. You always can choose not to exercise your rights under the loan documents, but if you don't have protections in place, then you have no options.

Even still, proceed under the assumption that if anything could go wrong, it will go wrong—at the worst time and in the worst way. Protect yourself with the ability to take back the business in case of default (if you don't want to take back the business, such a provision provides no additional security), personal guarantees from the buyer if he has large net worth, and other measures that protect your interests. If the buyer also has third-party financing, the third party will usually require seller financing be subordinated to their security interests.

If it fits your personal financial plan, providing seller financing will strengthen and expedite the deal in several ways. For example, granting a loan for part of the sales price will:

- Give you considerably more leverage in the negotiations
- Reassure the buyer that you are confident in the long-term success of the business
- Discourage the buyer from searching for ways to reduce the sale price accepted by both parties in the LOI
- Make it easier for the buyer to come up the cash needed to close
- Accelerate the closing process by avoiding the delays associated with a commercial bank loan or an SBA-backed loan
- Reduce loan origination fees (no points) for the buyer and provide more flexible terms and conditions than a commercial bank
- Spread your proceeds from the sale over several tax years, which often reduces the overall tax liability

Of course, you will earn above-market interest on the loan. To reward the seller for accepting the added risk of financing, the interest rate on a seller-financed loan is generally higher than a commercial bank would charge—but not high enough to make the buyer complain.

Obviously, when you agree to a seller-financed loan you sweeten the deal for the buyer, but you also accept two huge risks. First, the buyer may default on loan payments, which happens all too often. If the buyer loses customers, mismanages operations, fails to manage cash flow, or the market tanks, then making monthly or quarterly payments to you is likely to be among the buyer's first cuts. Therefore, you must secure your interests with multi-layered protections. Second, the provisions you put into the loan agreement may be insufficient to recover your losses. For example, the agreement for seller financing may contain a proviso that allows you to take control of the company if the buyer defaults on loan payments, management fees, or earn-outs. However, the company's income-producing assets (e.g., employees, inventory, and equipment) most likely will be depleted before you can legally regain control of the company. An alternative to a regular loan is to receive preferred equity. As an owner you have more legal rights regarding management of the company. However, the returns you earn generally aren't deductible, and you will be subordinated to all other creditors.

The choice to grant a seller-financed loan should not be taken lightly. It's all too common to negotiate a sweetheart deal, but not receive all of the proceeds. Under the best of circumstances, seller financing is risky. Work very closely with your attorney to develop an enforceable loan agreement, and request several forms of collateral to maximize your options for recovering the loan balance. Some buyers and sellers use preferred equity with a stated or variable dividend rate instead of a seller loan. Preferred equity gives the buyer flexibility on payments, and offers the seller the possibility of enhanced returns.

The top level of collateral, of course, is the business and the assets it owns. Second, if possible, secure the loan with unrelated buyer-owned assets that could be seized and sold if the buyer defaults on payments. The third level of collateral is a personal guarantee from the buyer and his spouse. Again, your rights probably will be subordinated to third-party lenders and, in fact, you might be prohibited from exercising your rights by the lender until the lender is paid. In the final analysis, the most effective way to protect your interests is to insist on a large cash payment at closing and minimize the amount of seller financing. That way, if the buyer defaults and you take the business back, you at least will have cash to rebuild the company and sell it all over again!

MISTAKE #38

AFRAID TO SAY *NO*

Whether it is issuing an ultimatum, walking away from the deal, or some other strong-armed tactic, an experienced negotiator knows when to play hardball.

After five months of intense negotiations and two extensions of the exclusionary period, it seemed that the deal to sell Dick's company was finally ready to close. Due diligence and development of the Purchase & Sale Agreement were essentially done, and closing was scheduled for the following week. Everybody thought all the issues had been resolved when the buyer dropped a bomb—he cut the price by a million dollars and justified his action by saying that the company's performance since the LOI was signed had been below projections.

Dick was devastated. The deal didn't work for him financially at the lower price. On the other hand, it would be awkward to back out of the deal. The employees had been briefed (most were shareholders who also were affected by the price cut), and the management team had begun to align with the new owner. Dick's wife said: *"Just say NO. The company has survived many crises in its twenty-two-year life, and it will survive this one too."* So Dick told the buyer the deal wouldn't happen at the lower price. The transaction closed at the original price two weeks later.

When Dick discussed the matter with his advisors, they chuckled and said that it was the textbook negotiation strategy called *nibbling:* ask for more concessions until the other party says *NO*. The equity investor who bought Dick's company negotiated several deals a year, while this was only the second transaction in Dick's lifetime. Dick was a neophyte in a world of highly experienced negotiators; they just wanted to see how far they could push Dick before he would say *NO*.

There is a crossroad in most negotiations when hardball tactics are necessary to close the deal. Whether it is using competition, issuing an ultimatum, walking from the deal, or some other strong-armed tactic, an experienced negotiator knows the right time to play hardball. In M&A deals, selling price is often a lightning rod for hard-nosed negotiations. Buyers see asking price as little more than a place to begin negotiating. When you have a professional appraisal or can cite a widely recognized valuation formula, you are less likely to receive a lowball offer. But you should still expect to be flexible with regard to the selling price.

There are no fixed rules for what buyers should offer, or what offers should be rejected. That being said, when a buyer who is financially qualified and knowledgeable about your industry makes an offer within 20 percent of your asking price, your broker should meet with the buyer to discuss the price differential and related matters. If the offer is below that number, it still may be appropriate to make a counteroffer with the intention of walking away if the buyer doesn't come back with a more reasonable offer. Negotiating doesn't mean giving away your business. Rather, it means considering each sincere offer in terms of its price and structure. A low price with a tax-advantaged structure and favorable payment terms in the end may yield higher net proceeds.

The tax consequences of a transaction are just as important as price since the buyer and seller both want to maximize their after-tax returns. Unfortunately, deal structures that reduce your tax liability usually have adverse tax consequences for the buyer, and vice versa. Balancing price and tax considerations requires open-minded negotiation with the buyer. After closing an asset sale, the price and allocation among asset classes will be reported to the IRS on Form 8594. This is a complex matter, so you definitely will need professional tax and financial planning advice to negotiate and accept a final price, a price allocation, and payment terms.

Allocation of the sale price to the asset classes shown on IRS Form 8594 affects the tax liabilities for both parties. The seller will want to recapture previously claimed depreciation tax deductions at ordinary income rates based on the asset class. The asset class determines the length of time over which the buyer can depreciate or amortize the assets. The somewhat subjective and highly negotiable allocations occur in a pre-defined order using fair market value of the assets. For example, the value of your company's cash and cash equivalents is recorded in the first asset class, and that amount is subtracted from the sale price. The process repeats for each succeeding class until the sale price is fully allocated. Any amount that isn't allocated to one of the top six classes goes into goodwill. The seven asset classes specified on IRS Form 8594 in order of precedence are:

- Class I, Cash and Cash-Equivalents, includes cash on hand and in checking, money market, and savings accounts.
- Class II, Marketable Securities, includes government securities, certificates of deposit, stocks, bonds, and foreign currencies.
- Class III, Mark-to-Market Assets, includes accounts receivable, loans receivable, debt instruments, and stock warrants.
- Class IV, Stock-in-Trade, is mainly inventory. Buyers prefer this class because it quickly turns into tax-deductible expenses.
- Class V, Tangible Assets, includes buildings, furniture, equipment, fixtures, land, vehicles, and leasehold improvements at fair market value. Again, buyers like this class because it is usually depreciable over three to five years.
- Class VI, Intangible Assets, includes non-physical assets used for business operations such as: intellectual property, workforce-in-place, proprietary processes, permits, trademarks, Internet sites, and covenants not-to-compete. Some intangible assets are not depreciable because they do not have a useful life, but generally such assets are depreciable over an extended period.
- Class VII, Goodwill. Sellers want to allocate as much of the price as possible to goodwill because it is taxed at the capital gains rate. Conversely, this is the worst class from a buyer's perspective since it has the longest tax write-off period (generally fifteen years).

If the price allocation or payment structure causes serious tax liabilities, you may want to negotiate a lower price, a more favorable structure for the deal, or alternative ways for the buyer to compensate you.

Consulting and non-compete agreements can serve as a relief valve in tense price negotiations. Naturally, the buyer wants to be certain that you won't compete with him after you leave the company, and thereby reduce the value of the goodwill he just bought from you. Decisions in this area usually are documented in a not-to-compete agreement, along with a consulting agreement or employment agreement for which the buyer will compensate the seller. In some cases, the IRS may rule that consulting agreements without real services are actually payments for goodwill and insist that they be amortized over fifteen years.

Normally, the buyer will ask you to sign a non-compete agreement, but will allocate only a small part of the price to the agreement because it is amortized over fifteen years even though the term of the agreement may be much shorter. You, on the other hand, would like as much of the sale price as is reasonable to be allocated to a non-compete agreement since proceeds are taxed as capital gains. The specific terms of a non-compete agreement are negotiable, and depend on what you intend to do after closing professionally. In Dick's case, for example, the term of the non-compete agreement was five years, and none of the sale price was allocated to the agreement. The agreement specified that Dick could not market or perform work for any of his company's customers, and he was prohibited from soliciting the company's employees. On the other hand, the agreement allowed Dick to consult with companies in the same industry and serve as a member of their Board of Directors.

If the buyer wants your help after closing and you are willing to stick around for a while, the buyer will offer you a management consulting or employment contract. Payments under such contracts can offset a price reduction. The buyer will want to pay you as much as possible under the contract because the payments are tax-deductible business expenses. For you, on the other hand, such payments are taxed as ordinary income rather than capital gains. If you accept employment as part of your deal, negotiate tax-free benefits like company-paid health and life insurance to offset higher taxes. Finally, ensure the services you are expected to deliver and the amount you will be paid are clearly specified.

In closing, remember the objective of the negotiations is to close the deal. That means sometimes you will need to make compromises and, at other times, hardball tactics may be appropriate. Consider the buyer's propositions carefully and remain flexible because, as discussed above, there are many degrees of freedom in closing the gap between what you want for your company and what the buyer is willing to pay.

MISTAKE #39

OH WHAT A DAY!

An M&A deal is like a thunderstorm—except when the storm ends, there really is a pot of gold at the end of the rainbow!

A CEO who had sold his company suggested that Dick visit an ATM on closing day after the electronic transfers were completed. He liked the idea. After closing, Dick and his wife rushed to their bank, entered their password, selected balance inquiry, and were stunned by what they saw. Mentally, they knew what the balance would be, but seeing the number on the ATM left them breathless. It made the twenty-two-year struggle to build the business and ten-month brawl to sell it seem worthwhile. Even though the money was gone the next day for the mortgage, debts, investments, and family members, seeing the number on the ATM screen is a sweet memory. We hope you have that experience!

In the entire life of your company, no day will be like closing day when you give control of *your* company to the buyer. The Purchase & Sale Agreement will put a value on the business you spent many years creating, and specify how you will be paid for your efforts. Even in a simple closing, there will be many documents for you and the buyer to sign to seal the deal. Your attorney will guide you through the signings, and ensure the "Ts" are crossed and the "Is" are dotted. You also may sign a promissory note, employment agreement, bulk sales agreement, minutes for Board meetings, lease transfers, among other documents. In Dick's deal, for example, the last document signed was a release from the landlord who agreed to transfer the office lease to the new owner.

The "Source & Uses of Funds Document," also called a settlement sheet, is among the most significant. That document shows all financial details related to closing including: the sale price, price adjustments, loan proceeds, and costs to be paid by you, the buyer, or someone else (sources of funds); and amounts to be distributed to you, the buyer, and others (uses of funds). "Price adjustments" may be related to the value of inventory, accounts receivable, accounts payable, and other working capital items on closing day. "Other costs" includes items like legal fees, escrow fees, broker fees, and prorated expenses. Of the utmost importance, the settlement sheet shows exactly how much cash will be wired to your account or given to you in a certified check. Normally, the buyer's attorney will prepare a draft settlement sheet, everyone on both sides of the table will review it, and the buyer and you will approve it to avoid unpleasant surprises at closing. Don't be alarmed if the settlement sheet changes several times a day in the week before closing.

As soon as possible after closing, formally announce the sale to your employees even if they already know about it. Positively don't let them hear about the sale through the rumor mill, or worse yet, in a newspaper or media message. If possible, host an all-hands meeting to publish the news. Make it clear that the business has been sold, tell them about the buyer, and reassure them that their positions and compensation are safe. Also tell employees whether you will remain with the company and, if so, for how long and in what capacity. Remind them that it's important to keep the news under wraps for a few days until the buyer and you can discuss the news with customers, suppliers, and strategic partners.

Practice the presentation so you can maintain composure. Expect it to be emotional—after all, these people worked long and hard to make the company a success. Don't even think about announcing the news in an e-mail! First, an impersonal e-mail won't answer the *what-is-in-it-for-me* questions that will be on the employees' minds; and second, the e-mail will be instantly forwarded to outsiders. Sellers often announce the sale to employees with the buyer present, introduce the buyer, and then leave so the new owner can speak alone with *his* employees.

In writing this book, we asked each CEO, CFO, broker, lawyer, and CPA who gave us a story: "*In your experience, what percent of signed LOIs produce a closed deal?*" Of the twenty or so M&A professionals who answered, the responses ranged from 60 to 90 percent—those are good odds. But in the words of Yogi Berra, the Hall of Fame baseball player, remember after you sign an LOI, "*It's not over til it's over.*" So manage your business operations from that perspective. That being said, we'd love to meet you at an ATM on the day your deal closes!

CHAPTER FOUR

GETTING THE DEAL
DONE AS THE BUYER

Finding a seller and signing a Letter of Intent (LOI) is a big milestone, but that doesn't make it a done deal. You still have big decisions to make—and lots of risks to face—before closing day.

The buyer and seller celebrated LOI signing after a vigorous limited auction, but the celebration was short-lived. Early in due diligence, the buyer found irregularities in how the seller handled some government contracts, specifically:

- Violations of the Buy American Act by using foreign materials in systems delivered to government agencies without a waiver
- Violations of the Service Contracts Act by paying employees less than the required minimum hourly wages
- Employees in non-exempt positions misclassified as exempt from the Fair Labor Standards Act and not paid for overtime

Like many small businesses, in most cases the seller wasn't familiar with the requirements of these and other federal regulations.

On the other hand, the buyer was a large, publicly-traded company that was extremely concerned about its public image (the so-called "headlines risk"). It saw large risks in these irregularities:

- Liabilities for back wages and government contract overcharges
- The potential for adverse, damaging publicity
- Overstated profits in the seller's income statement and projections

Because of these risks, the buyer asked the seller to fix the irregularities before continuing with due diligence, whereupon the seller withdrew from the transaction and took itself off the market.

In the unpredictable M&A world, the deal you are just beginning to discuss today with a potential seller has roughly a one-in-ten chance of producing a closed transaction. The odds increase to about two-in-three when an LOI is signed, but there are many explosive issues during due diligence and negotiations that could destroy even a sure-shot deal. To maximize the odds of closing your deal (and at the same time reduce transaction costs), you need to understand your seller's motivations and M&A background. You can avoid many pitfalls by learning the answers to the following questions:

- Is this the seller's first transaction or is he an M&A veteran?
- Who did the seller hire to represent him? And why?
- How important are price, timing, and cash at closing to him?
- Is the seller fully prepared for due diligence and negotiations?
- Does the seller want to protect and reward his key employees?
- How much weight does the seller place on values and culture?
- What will it take to gain the seller's trust?

If you are uncomfortable with the seller's answers to these questions, it may be wise to simply walk away and look for another deal. Avoid the natural inclination to go through with a transaction just because of the effort, time, and resources you have already invested in it.

As the buyer, the roller-coaster ride begins when you find a business that matches your target criteria, then sign an LOI that places a value on a company which, in reality, you know little about. The ride ends when the Purchase & Sale Agreement (or equivalent) is signed by all parties, and the initial funds transfers are completed. Or it ends when the deal falls apart. To avoid the latter outcome, you will need to:

- Learn everything you can about what you are buying
- Determine the real value of what you are buying
- Avoid misunderstandings that can kill an otherwise good deal
- Decide how the seller's business will be integrated with yours
- Deal with unexpected revelations in a professional manner

The last item is particularly vital because the unexpected arises, well, when you least expect it! During the very intense and often frustrating negotiations that you will experience, remember that your objective is to close the deal—assuming it's a good deal for you as the buyer.

MISTAKE #40

NOT SELLING THE SELLER

As the buyer, sell the benefits of your company to the seller as strongly as he is selling his company to you.

The owners of two software development companies were friends that often worked together on projects as subcontractors to one another. The owner of one company thought the companies would be perfect for a merger. The second company had two owners. One was the President who was a technologist and ran the company on a daily basis, while the other seemed to be merely a silent partner. Their company faced several challenges: It was undercapitalized, lacked effective project managers other than the President, and had an erratic sales program.

The owner of the first company casually mentioned the concept of a merger to the joint owners. After all, the two companies' projects could be integrated easily, and they could use their expensive technical staffs more efficiently. In addition, his company was growing rapidly, highly profitable, and had a strong management team and an experienced sales manager who could market both companies. The two owners liked the concept, but couldn't decide what they might want out of a deal.

Over the next two years, the owner of the first company increased the intensity and frequency of the merger discussions with the joint owners. He also researched their company's financial condition and reputation with customers. For example, their Dunn & Bradstreet (D&B) reports showed deteriorating credit ratings. His repetitive offers were received politely, but with little authentic interest.

Then the silent partner decided to retire, so the President bought his stock and ran the company alone. Business seemed to improve at first. The President extended his hours in the office; soon sales, revenue, and profits increased. The owner of the first company thought the merger idea was dead, but he mentioned it one more time to the President. The response was shocking—he accepted the offer! Seems the President was burned out because of the intensified workload and loss of support from the silent partner. The deal closed two months later and, as expected, the merged organization was spectacularly successful.

By all rights, the last merger attempt should have failed just like the earlier tries. But the emotional strain on the President made it the right time for him to sell. This point is, until the time is right in the seller's eyes, any attempt to buy will fail. Nevertheless, building rapport with an owner of a target company is an effective buy strategy. In this case, the buyer built a strong relationship with owners of the target company, and was persistent (but informal) in guiding them toward a sale.

For example, the buyer didn't bring an attorney into the deal until the President said *YES* to the idea of a transaction. Sometimes, a buyer will use an attorney in early discussions, which can scare a seller and kill a possible deal before it is even alive. On the other hand, it is appropriate to consult your attorney and CPA before discussing a price, payment terms, or other conditions of an LOI—especially if the buyer is an M&A novice. Nothing can squelch a deal faster than a surprise in the LOI that should have been discussed in advance with the seller.

Sometimes, you will find yourself in a limited auction where you are not the low bidder but you've gone as high as you can in the price. The first thing to look at is after-tax proceeds to the seller. Stuart has saved many deals in this predicament with creative, win-win tax planning approaches. Ask your attorney and CPA if there are ways to split the tax savings and offer a better deal to the seller. However, you many need to help the seller understand how alternative deal structures actually increase his after-tax proceeds. Even if you can't match your opponent's price, your creativity may gain you favor with the seller.

Furthermore, you can still win the deal by selling the seller on your company. Many deals don't go to the highest bidder. Sometimes, sellers value the best fit for employees, continuity in customer relationships, and business philosophies over a few percentage points in price. So keep trying. In a competitive situation, you should become the seller and win the bid using factors other than price, such as:

- Your financial ability to close the deal
- Your knowledge of and contacts in the industry
- Your reputation for post-closing integrity
- The after-closing role that you offer to the seller
- How you integrate the seller's managers into your team
- Your genuine high regard for the seller's employees
- Compatibility between the two corporate cultures

You may want to introduce the seller to sellers from past deals you have closed. Also, encourage him to look past the money to see the chemistry between your companies, opportunities for his employees and managers, and your track record in closing deals and delivering on promises.

Another factor that can sway the seller's decision to pick your offer over higher offers is your company's size. There are tradeoffs between selling to a large or small company. If your company is larger than your competitors, highlight your stability (including the performance of your publicly-traded stock, if applicable), your extensive financial resources and customer base, the range of opportunities for the seller's employees, and the perfect spot you have for the seller's operations within your organization. And, of course, a small company has fewer resources, so there is a much higher probability that your small competitor will not be able to secure the financing required to close the deal.

On the other hand, if your company is smaller than other buyers, you will want to tout your management agility, a better cultural fit, how close your executives are to employees and customers, and less red tape in closing the deal. If your financing is secure, show the commitment documents to the seller. Your large-company competitors actually may provide evidence during LOI negotiations to prove your point that a small company is a better, less bureaucratic choice.

In any case, the importance of selling the seller doesn't end when the LOI is signed. Opportunities to sell your company continue during due diligence, negotiating the Purchase & Sale Agreement, and planning the integration. At all costs, be sure that you and your team avoid *bad-buyer behaviors* like criticizing employees, a pure numbers focus, aloofness, minimizing the seller's accomplishments, or telling the seller that he owns an "ugly baby." Such behaviors will quickly un-sell most sellers.

MISTAKE #41

LETTING PRICE
KILL A GOOD DEAL

*If your target is a valuable strategic acquisition, be
creative in finding ways to close the price gap between
what the seller is asking and what you are willing to pay.*

At the height of the market in fall of 2007, an equity firm raised
capital to finance a health care IT roll-up that would target long-term
contracts with federal agencies. Quickly, two companies were found
that met the acquisition criteria and they issued a LOI to each one offering all
cash. In initial discussions, they led each CEO to believe he would lead the
roll-up. Since the CEOs knew each other, that slipup caused confusion and
delayed both acquisitions. As the negotiations dragged on, market conditions
deteriorated and valuations fell.

With the economy in freefall, investors withdrew from the venture capital
fund and the equity firm had to modify its offers in spring 2008 because it no
longer had enough cash for the transactions. Even though both companies
continued their growth, the new offers were 20 percent lower overall, with
only 60 percent in cash with the balance in preferred stock and stock options
in the roll-up company. When both of the CEOs insisted on all cash, the deals
fell through. Two lessons here. First, it is almost always fatal for the buyer
to widen the price gap or change the transaction basis during the deal. And
second, things always seem to get worse when a transaction is delayed.

In another transaction, a strategic buyer proposed an asset sale in the
LOI but, as is typical, the seller wanted a stock sale. The real issue was
that the buyer intended to merge operations with his existing company and
lay off most of the seller's staff. The buyer was concerned about potential legal problems with the layoffs (several employees were in protected
groups which could subject the buyer to costly litigation), and he wanted

the seller to underwrite that liability and establish a substantial escrow to defend against lawsuits. They found a creative solution: The transaction was structured to liquidate the seller's company prior to the sale. The seller announced that he was shutting down his company and paid all employees a severance bonus, including certain employees who were later rehired by the buyer. The buyer bought the seller's inventory, contracts, building, and equipment at a reduced price that covered a portion of the severance bonuses. Everybody walked away happy from the deal, with no escrows and no lawsuits.

Don't let a price gap be a deal-killer. Be creative in finding ways to close the gap between what the seller wants and what you are willing to pay. Stock-only transactions once were common, but today they are rare because of the availability of low-cost debt and the possibility that the seller may be required to pay taxes on the stock without the cash to pay them. Sellers generally prefer an all-cash deal, and if everybody could agree on the price, it would be the easiest approach for buyers too.

Unfortunately, in the real world sellers and buyers seldom agree on a value for the company being sold. The so-called *Endowment Syndrome* causes sellers to see a rosy future and ask for more than buyers, who see both real and imaginary threats, are willing to pay. Therefore, the norm today is part cash at closing with the balance paid incrementally after closing under various devices. Two common devices, for example, are: (1) escrows to protect the buyer from downside uncertainties; and (2) earn-outs to reward the seller for upside gains that materialize while at the same time shielding the buyer from risks in those areas.

Studies confirm that buyers earn a higher return-on-investment when payments to the seller are contingent on future performance than in all-cash deals or stock-swaps. The returns are enhanced further when the seller and/or the seller's management team remain with the business for a year or longer. Therefore, consider earn-outs and other contingent payments in your transaction as a mechanism to incentivize the seller and simultaneously reduce your downside risk. Furthermore, as a savvy buyer you should be able to explain to your Board why the price you paid was a fair market value—earn-outs and other contingent payments help you to do that.

Be flexible when negotiating the Purchase & Sale Agreement. By restructuring the deal, you can usually offer a higher price or higher net proceeds to the seller while at the same time reducing risks, increasing upside potential, and minimizing the cash required at closing. It may be useful to channel your thinking into the following four categories when searching for creative devices to close the price gap in ways that would be acceptable to the seller:

- *Contingent Payments.* Earn-outs, a common form of contingent payment, pay the seller additional amounts when favorable events happen, such as renewing a large contract, winning a competitive award, or realizing a specified revenue level. Another example is "convertible debt," where the seller, at his option, converts part or all of seller financing into stock that the buyer redeems according to a performance algorithm in the Purchase & Sale Agreement. A third variant is a "participatory note," where the seller finances the deal at a variable interest rate—say 6 percent as the interest floor with step increases up to 12 percent based on margins or revenue growth. Except for earn-outs, these devices are cheap for the buyer, since payments are deductible in the year that the interest is paid.

- *Escrows and Holdbacks.* Representations and warranties regarding future events can protect you against downside risks by allowing you to recover part of the purchase price if an untoward event occurs or an expected event fails to materialize. In escrows, cash is withheld from closing and deposited with an escrow agent. Under conditions specified in a written agreement, the cash is distributed to the buyer or the seller at predetermined intervals. In a holdback, the buyer reduces the cash at closing by a specified amount that is subject to future distribution to the buyer if certain targets (e.g., employee retention or gross margins) are met. A holdback is more advantageous to the buyer than an earn-out because it reduces the cash to be deposited in escrows at closing (assuming earn-outs are deposited in escrow). Alternatively, allowing the buyer to offset seller financing, consulting, or other deferred payments in effect creates another post-closing escrow.

- *Tax-Advantaged Concessions.* As the buyer, you are permitted to step up the tax basis of most assets you acquire, thus producing a large depreciation and amortization shield against future income taxes. Subject to limitations, net operating loss (NOL) carry-forwards and debt tax shields have similar benefits, as do employment and consulting agreements with the seller.

- *Cash and Cash Equivalents.* There is no return-on-investment from buying cash, cash equivalents, or receivables. So, in return for a lower price, let the seller keep cash and cash equivalents, such as accounts receivable, notes receivable, and certificates of deposit. It may be advantageous for the seller to use the cash to pay dividends that currently would be taxed at favorable capital gains tax rates. In addition, like a real estate transaction, payment of closing costs such as legal fees and transfer taxes on assets are negotiable.

Of course, these ideas are just the tip of the iceberg of what is possible in each of the four categories. Look for other possibilities that uniquely fit conditions of the transaction you are negotiating.

As the closing date approaches, the concept of handing over a pile of Ben Franklins to the seller is acceptable if his asking price is reasonable and his business is threat-free. However, when price negotiations freeze up, contingent payments and other creative techniques are the next best thing to greenbacks to thaw them out. As the buyer, in the week or so before closing, you will have more leverage than at any other time in the process because it would be exceedingly difficult and embarrassing for the seller to back out of the deal at such a late date. However, when used in a creative, win-win manner, techniques like those mentioned above could be the difference between closing the deal at a price you can live with, or losing the deal with no return on the investment of your time and your transaction expenses.

MISTAKE #42

UNVERIFIED OPTIMISM

Believe what the buyer tells you about his company
and its future, but verify those beliefs by conducting due
diligence as if you are looking for a needle in a haystack.

The leader of the buyer's due diligence team began the process with a meeting in the office of the seller's CPA. Everything appeared to be in perfect order based on annual audits the CPA performed for the firm for eleven consecutive years. So the leader directed the due diligence team to focus its effort on legal matters, human resources, and operations.

However, audits don't tell the whole story. Audit standards require a statistical sampling of transactions, not a 100 percent review. Moreover, audits are conducted based on materiality standards: Transactions under a certain dollar value generally aren't reviewed. Therefore, misreporting a large number of similar low-value transactions might go undiscovered but collectively have a material effect on a company's financial position. Furthermore, auditors tend to examine balance sheet accounts in more detail than income and expense accounts. They focus on questions like:

- Does cash reconcile?
- Are receivables collectable?
- Are assets valued appropriately for the market?
- Is inventory valued correctly?
- Are billings accurate, complete, and timely?

Everything was in order relative to those questions, and no due diligence issues came up in the notes accompanying the audit reports.

The seller was a systems installation company. System components usually were drawn from inventory, but sometimes a customer provided components directly to the seller. Quite by accident, a junior member of the operations due diligence team saw that the quantity in inventory for a few high-value stock items was higher than the computerized records. Further investigation revealed that the computer system always charged a project for materials, even if they were customer-furnished. Of course, that error over-stated inventory costs and understated profits.

Normally, you wouldn't think that understating profits and inventory quantities would be an issue. However, when the income statement was recast, the seller pushed to increase the price using the multiplier in the LOI. On the other hand, the seller was concerned about the accounting procedures: *If we found one serious error, what else is there that we haven't found yet?* The buyer refused to increase the price from the offer in the LOI. The deal stalled and eventually fell apart.

There are lessons here for both buyers and sellers. On the buyer side, clean audits don't mean perfect accounting records and procedures. Audits should not substitute for thorough due diligence. Look at the materiality standards set by the auditor and during due diligence do your own statistical sampling of certain types of high-volume, low-value transactions to ensure there are no material distortions. On the seller side, the lesson learned is: favorable events and discoveries during due diligence rarely increase the price in the LOI—although they may be useful bargaining chips later in the negotiations. The LOI price should be considered a maximum, and due diligence findings can only reduce the price from the number accepted by both sides in the LOI.

We recommend you prepare a written due diligence plan, and assign the evaluation of each topic to a specific member of the team. Plan and conduct due diligence to achieve three essential objectives:

(1) Ensure there are no financial, legal, HR, or operational issues that threaten the company's future or your return-on-investment.

(2) Ensure the business is in the financial and operational condition that the seller claims it to be.

(3) Develop a plan to integrate the seller's finances and operations with yours after closing.

Generic due diligence checklists are available on the Internet at nominal cost, or you can ask your CPA or attorney for one. Financial statements that you receive prior to signing the LOI are useful in targeting areas to investigate. Among other things, you'll want to examine any ratios that are significantly better or worse than industry norms, and double-check accounts that are missing or unusual for the industry. In addition to the balance sheet and the income statement, the seller's statement of adjusted earnings and statement of cash flow are helpful in planning your due diligence effort. In particular, the statement of adjusted earnings is a gold mine of due diligence topics because it flags items that the seller considers to be unusual or non-recurring in his operations. Each of those is worth a thorough evaluation.

If you don't find something in due diligence you didn't expect, then you probably haven't looked deeply enough in all of the right places. Inevitably, there will be surprises. In selling his company, for example, Dick was surprised how much emphasis the buyer put on government audit findings. Next to contract compliance and human resources, it was the area where the buyer's due diligence team spent the most time. They also ran background checks on senior managers, even though most of them held active government security clearances. They were looking, of course, for "bad stuff" like contract overruns, conflicts of interest, lost customers, noncompliance issues, violations of federal regulations, and potential government claims. Their main objective was to know the true value of the company they were buying—and that should be on top of your priority list too.

Remain optimistic during the frustration and uncertainty of due diligence and negotiations, because the deal is likely to end shortly after you lose your patience or your optimism. That being said, however, unverified optimism can be fatal if you as a buyer see more opportunity than is substantiated by hard financial numbers, or expect more synergy than can be achieved after the deal is closed. Unrealistic optimism may be produced by several things: for example, the euphoria of beating a competitor in a hotly contested auction, an overly rosy view of industry growth, exciting but unproven cross-selling opportunities, or dubious projections for sales of a new technology.

Furthermore, unrealistic optimism may cause a buyer to overlook obvious red flags in due diligence or avoid looking in areas where they might find bad news. If that happens, the buyer is likely to pay too much for the company and naively believe that he can run the company better than the seller. When there are several significant red flags, don't be afraid to talk with the seller about changing the price, or adding more warranties and higher escrows. While closing the deal is obviously paramount, Stuart warns his clients: *"Some of the best deals you make are the ones that you don't make."* Don't throw good money after bad by continuing an acquisition solely because of transaction costs you may have incurred to date.

Sometimes, the seller will complicate due diligence by providing the minimum information required to answer your questions, thereby hiding data that might point you toward areas of risk or weakness. Since LOIs frequently specify a fixed time period for due diligence, sellers also may intentionally or unintentionally delay delivering information that might be perceived negatively, hoping the due diligence time period will expire before the bad news is discovered. Therefore, if the seller delays giving you the information you request, be concerned and increase the level of due diligence. Also, you may want the LOI to provide for automatic extensions of the due diligence if the seller fails to provide information in a timely manner. Unfortunately, if you discover additional risks or other bad news after due diligence or closing, your recourse may be limited. Believe the seller and be optimistic about the future of his company, but verify everything that he claims and leave no stone unturned in your search to find the true value of the company you are about to buy.

MISTAKE #43

PENNY WISE
AND POUND FOOLISH

*Don't fall into the trap of thinking you know the seller
and can get by with little or no operational due diligence.*

The seller and buyer worked together on several projects over a four-year period. Sometimes one company, and then the other, would be the prime contractor. When one company voiced an interest in buying the second company, the seller quickly accepted. They negotiated price and terms, and an LOI was signed in roughly a week. The buyer retained his CPA and attorney to conduct financial, legal, and human resources due diligence but said: "*I know this company, so let's skip operational due diligence to save time and money.*" Besides, he had no one on staff with the experience to critically examine the seller's business operations.

Due diligence was routine, and the few issues found were quickly resolved. The Purchase & Sale Agreement was signed by both parties within the thirty-day exclusionary period. Unfortunately, three months after closing the buyer lost two key customers because of quality issues and strained relationships he didn't know about. These two customers were nearly 25 percent of total revenue, but there were no provisions in the agreement to allow the buyer to recover a portion of the sale price for post-closing customer losses.

In another case, the transaction was conducted hastily (three months start to finish) because investors were pushing the buyer to close a deal. The buyer hired his CPA and used his staff for due diligence. One of the seller's contracts (40 percent of annual revenue) expired just six months after closing. Incredibly, the due diligence team missed it. They called the seller's customers, but asked superficial questions like: "*Are you satisfied with the services you receive?*" They didn't ask about contract renewal provisions. Fortunately, the buyer won the re-competition, but at lower margins. Had he known about the re-competition, the buyer would have inserted earn-outs in the Purchase & Sale Agreement to recover part of the sale price to make up for the lower margins.

Financial due diligence always gets the most attention, and legal and HR due diligence aren't far behind. But operational due diligence (e.g., customers, employees, products and services, and the business pipeline) frequently gets shortchanged. The odds are one-in-three that you will be negotiating with a company that you have done business with in the past, and better than nine-in-ten that you will purchase a company in your industry. But don't let that familiarity push you into the folly of thinking you know the company or its unique niche in your industry.

Another common mistake is using inexperienced people to perform due diligence because they are more available—and perhaps more affordable—than your most qualified people. Unfortunately, junior people often miss obvious red flags while a seasoned due diligence professional acts like a detective—a Lieutenant Columbo-like questioner who asks several people the same question and analyzes differences in their answers to find issues. On the other extreme, a due diligence conducted like a grand inquisition can adversely affect the attitude of the seller's staff toward the buyer. If you don't have the talent available for thorough operational due diligence, hire a consultant who knows your industry and understands M&A transactions. A seasoned professional will soften questions of the seller's employees and records. In any case, don't shortchange operational due diligence.

As buyer, you'll want to investigate the following operational areas:

- *Business Model.* How does the seller's business operate? Will it run smoothly after he leaves? Evaluate the seller's organizational chart and operations manual to understand production and delivery processes, and ensure they will transfer when you are the owner.
- *Customer Base.* How loyal are the seller's customers, and are they loyal to him or the company? Is the customer base growing? Who are key customers, and how long have they been customers? What were the buying patterns of the key customers over the preceding two years? How do customers rate the company's performance?
- *Billing Practices and Contracts.* How much does the seller charge, and how are billings handled? What are the margins, and are they

sustainable? When was the last price increase and how did it affect sales? How firm is the backlog, and is it expanding? Is the seller in compliance with applicable government regulations?

- *Sales and Marketing.* What is the seller's growth strategy? How well does it work? What are the company's strengths and weaknesses versus its competitors? What is the marketing and sales process? How large is the business development pipeline, and is it growing or shrinking? What large opportunities are on the horizon? Are there seasonal peaks/valleys in sales and revenue?

- *Staff.* Is the company staffed with full-time, part-time, or freelance workers? How long has each employee been with the company? Which employees have employment agreements? How many positions are vacant, and how are employees recruited? What policies are used to retain employees, and how does the seller's retention rate compare to industry norms? Does the company comply with employment laws?

- *Production and Service Delivery.* How does the company produce and deliver its products and services (including computer systems, software, and equipment)? Does the seller hold clear, transferable rights for the intellectual property it uses? Are agreements with subcontractors, suppliers, and distributors easily transferable?

- *Disputes, Litigation, and Audits.* Does the company have any open disputes with customers or suppliers? If yes, what is their status? How does the company resolve customer complaints to maintain positive relationships and avoid litigation? Is the company subject to government audits? What were findings in previous audits and were they resolved?

Of course, this general list of operational due diligence topics should be customized to your industry and the specific company you are buying.

One caution with respect to due diligence: don't get lost in historical numbers since projections for the future are more important. That being said, due diligence is an opportune time to analyze the strengths, weaknesses, opportunities, and threats (SWOT) of the organization. We recommend that a SWOT analysis be included in the operational due diligence report. Even if due diligence doesn't reveal any surprises, the SWOT report alone will justify the cost of the effort.

MISTAKE #44

RUNNING THE NEGOTIATIONS METER

Some advisors will push to close the deal quickly, while others will be thorough during due diligence and negotiations. Your best interests require a balance between both extremes.

When Dick's company was sold, the transaction required three sets of attorneys: a large firm to represent the equity buyer, a large firm to represent Dick's company, and Stuart to represent the family trust and Dick on a personal basis. During negotiations, the attorneys frequently negotiated issues using e-mails and phone calls. Usually, the discussions were not reviewed in advance with the three principal parties. So, even after the attorneys agreed, the agreements still had to be staffed through Dick and his company on the seller side, and executives on the buyer side. It wasn't unusual for one or both sides to disagree with parts of the attorneys' agreements, and the negotiation process would repeat itself.

That approach created an audit trail for negotiations, but it also kept the meter running on by-the-hour legal fees. Attorneys talking back-and-forth is expensive. The bill from each of the two large law firms was well into six digits. In addition, that approach slows the process and increases the risk of the deal blowing up. Stuart advises clients to control costs and keep the deal moving by having the buyer and seller to meet with each other (with their attorneys present) to resolve business issues after both sides have reviewed the issues and draft documents separately. Subsequent to the meeting, the attorneys can address the technical issues (if any) and document the agreements.

In another transaction, the minority partner in a small business made an offer to buy out the majority partner. Their personal relationship had deteriorated over the years, and they no longer wanted to work together. This relatively simple deal took over six months to negotiate and close, when it should have been done in one. Due diligence was unnecessary because the partners managed the business on a daily basis. However, during the transaction the two owners would discuss open points in the negotiations in the office that sometimes ended in angry arguments in front of employees. The outbursts damaged the business and it took weeks before the parties got back together to discuss the issues. Stuart, at their request and with appropriate conflict disclosures, represented both sides in the transaction. He acted as a mediator between the parties to protect the business. Given the anger during the negotiations, Stuart believes that if each partner had his own attorney, the deal might never have closed.

In small deals or deals between partners or friends, it is cost-effective to have a single attorney represent the company, mediate an agreement, and prepare neutral sale documents subject to appropriate conflict-of-interest disclosures. When the buyer and seller review the agreements, they may elect to retain a personal attorney to evaluate any controversial provisions. That approach controls costs, reduces conflict, and expedites the closing date by avoiding the need for several attorneys to participate in business negotiations or argue over boilerplate language that is of little consequence to either of the parties.

In every transaction, the buyer and seller require experienced M&A professionals they trust to get the deal done. Most transactions begin with the buyer and seller having an appreciation for each other's goals. But that feeling can evaporate quickly during hard-nosed negotiations. That's when professionals on both sides must calm tempers and use their resourcefulness to resolve complex issues. When you find out who will represent the seller, ask your attorney and CPA: *"Have you done a deal with them?"* If they have successfully closed previous transactions, you can be confident they will probably close yours too. On the other hand, if they lack respect for the other side, be prepared to pay for extra hours to reach an agreement.

Since they work for you, don't hesitate to establish guidelines for the roles your attorney and CPA will play in the transaction versus how you and your senior staff will participate. There are several open questions:

- What role will your attorney and CPA play in due diligence?
- What role (if any) will consultants play in due diligence?
- What role (if any) will your staff play in due diligence?
- When can your attorney represent you in meetings with the seller?

- When can your CPA represent you in meetings with the seller?
- What are the pivotal areas where you want to represent yourself?
- How will decisions be made regarding controversial matters?
- What are the deal-breakers for you? For the seller?

Since the answers to these questions depend on having a clear plan for conducting due diligence and negotiations, we recommend you hold a planning meeting shortly after the LOI is signed with everyone on your team.

It may be an effective strategy to ensure that your attorney negotiates only legal matters with the seller's representatives, and your CPA only participates in tax-related negotiations. However, the CPA and attorney must coordinate their actions to avoid giving the seller contradictory positions. As discussed above, when the subject is mainly a business matter, we recommend you hold a four-way meeting with the seller and your respective attorneys. You and the seller can discuss and decide the matter directly, while the attorneys provide advice when necessary and document decisions made during the meeting in the Purchase & Sale Agreement and other documents. One rule of thumb at such meetings: *Spend more time listening than talking.*

Keep in mind the perspectives of your hired professionals. Attorneys, CPAs, and consultants get paid by the hour *to be right.* So their focus is likely to cross the *T*s and dot the *I*s. Instruct those professionals that you would rather *get what you want than be technically correct.* If document reviews with your attorney show that the opposing counsel is focusing on minutia, you may want to have a side discussion with the seller to ensure that he understands that such legal work could cost both of you a lot of time and money. On the other hand, brokers are paid a success fee when the deal closes, so you can expect them to push everyone to make decisions and finish the negotiations. Your best interests usually lie in the middle of those two extremes.

Obviously, you want to control transaction costs, but due diligence and negotiations should not be cut short. Thoroughness, while costing more in the short term, is much less expensive than closing a bad deal. That being said, delays kill deals! Don't rush through a transaction, but at the same time ensure everyone maintains momentum toward closing.

MISTAKE #45

SKIMPY ESCROWS

Resist the seller's pressure to minimize the escrows. Increase the escrows if the seller hasn't been audited, if you receive sales or profit guarantees, or if there are other high-risk situations.

Escrows were the main negotiating issue during a transaction in one particular deal. As is typical, the buyer wanted more value reserved in escrow, and the seller wanted less. The seller strongly resisted escrows in any form, including a short-term escrow to be liquidated after an audit by the buyer's CPA. Such resistance should have been a red flag to the buyer, but he agreed reluctantly to accept 10 percent of the purchase price in a single escrow that had a two-part payout:

- Half to be paid after an audit of tangible net asset value
- Half for representations regarding the value of new business in the pipeline and other representations with a payout after one year

The seller operated on cash basis and had never been audited. Since the deal was a stock sale, all liabilities transferred to the buyer at closing.

The sale closed December 31st using the seller's internally-prepared financial statements. The audit performed by the buyer's CPA took sixty days and uncovered several accounting discrepancies including:

- Improper handling of deferred expenses
- Uncollectible accounts receivable and no allowance for bad debts
- Failure to recognize expenses incurred prior to the closing date
- A discrepancy in cash balance due to uncleared checks
- Under-amortization of leasehold improvements

The accounting discrepancies exceeded 7 percent of the sale price, which consumed most of the escrow. So when new sales in the pipeline failed to materialize, the escrow had insufficient funds to reimburse the buyer for recoveries specified in the purchase agreement. That left the buyer in the position of having to pursue the seller to recover additional damages due under the purchase agreement—often a tough process, but even more difficult here because the seller remained as an employee.

By comparison, the Stock Purchase Agreement for the sale of Dick's company established three separate escrow accounts, each governed by its own escrow agreement:

- *Balance Sheet Escrow,* which was liquidated ninety days after closing when the buyer's CPA audited the balance sheet to verify the net asset value claimed by Dick's company as of the closing date.
- *Representations Escrow* that protected the buyer against damages related to the seller's representations. It was liquidated a year after closing. The representations "bucket" was 1 percent of the sale price with a minimum claim size of $10,000.
- *Cash-to-Accrual Escrow.* The buyer's CPA calculated taxes due for the conversion from cash to accrual basis, and that amount was held in escrow to pay taxes due over four years as allowed by the IRS.

The first two escrows together were about 10 percent of the sale price, while the third escrow was the exact amount of the taxes due. The three escrows were administered and liquidated smoothly without any issues between the buyer and seller, largely because Dick's company had been audited for seven consecutive years prior to the sale.

The key lesson learned from these stories is *don't skimp on escrows.* If the seller has been audited for several consecutive years and there are no unusual contingencies, 10 percent escrow for a post-closing audit and representations is about right. Make the escrows higher if the seller has never been audited, if there is a guaranteed minimum for revenue and/or margins, or if there are other high-risk situations.

Escrows typically range from a low of 5 percent when the target is a large, well-managed company to a high of 20 percent of the purchase price when the target is a small, unaudited company. The escrow can be higher if it is the sole source for recovery of claims. Generally, escrows are held six months to three years depending on perceived risks, but in some cases the buyer may have the right to extend the escrow period when there is a good-faith basis for claims. Sub-accounts within a single escrow may be used to secure the buyer's interests relative to working capital deficiencies, revenue and profit guarantees, pending litigation, ongoing audits by government agencies, and other liabilities. As the buyer, if your company is large and well-capitalized, consider using holdbacks in lieu of escrows to reduce the cash required at closing.

Escrows usually are administered under a tri-party agreement among you, the seller, and an independent escrow agent. Funds are deposited in the escrow account at closing. You and the seller will follow guidelines provided in the escrow agreement when dealing with the escrow agent. The guidelines define responsibilities for you, the seller, and the escrow agent relative to release of funds, payment of taxes on account earnings, compensation for the agent, resolution of disputes, and liquidation of the account. If you don't skimp on the amount in the escrow, there should be more than enough in the account to cover your claims under terms of the purchase agreement.

An alternative to the use of escrows is offsets against other forms of deferred payments to the seller. For example, the buyer can be protected against breach of seller representations and warranties with reductions in payments due to the seller under consulting agreements, non-compete agreements, or seller financing. Of course, the offsets must be explicitly permitted according to the Purchase & Sale Agreement or the seller has valid reason to object. To protect both sides, buyer reductions generally are held in a separate escrow until the parties agree on the amount of the reduction, including the prevailing party's attorney fees. This provision serves to eliminate frivolous disagreements. Furthermore, such offsets may be red flags to the IRS relative to the current deductibility of the payments.

MISTAKE #46

SKIMMING OVER
THE AGREEMENTS

Negotiations require knowledge, thoroughness, and skill. If your negotiators are inexperienced, you're likely to pay for their on-the-job education...the expensive way.

The buyer and seller concluded negotiations and signed the Purchase & Sale Agreement, but because the price exceeded $50 million, closing was delayed pursuant the Hart-Scott-Rodino Act. That act requires a thirty-day exclusionary period for the Department of Justice (DOJ) to review the acquisition for possible anti-trust violations. Since the DOJ didn't object within the thirty-day window, which began when both parties signed the purchase agreement, the deal was approved by default and the funds were transferred to the seller.

The buyer negotiated representations and warranties in the purchase agreement to govern the seller's operations during the thirty-day window. One clause in particular required the seller to conduct business in a "normal manner," and not enter into any unusual agreements without the buyer's written approval. The seller, impatient to close a third-party contract related to the earn-outs, violated that representation by entering into a contract that precluded them (and their successors) from competing for new contracts with certain clients.

Two months after the deal officially closed, the buyer discovered the violation quite by accident when it submitted a proposal to an excluded customer, and the third party objected. After intense negotiations that nearly unraveled the deal, an economic settlement was reached wherein the buyer got a settlement from the escrow which, in effect, reduced the sale price. In this transaction, the buyer's team had extensive experience in negotiating agreements. For example, they knew the Hart-Scott-Rodino Act and how to handle it in a Purchase & Sale Agreement. Negotiations aren't the time to learn on the job. If your negotiators are inexperienced, you are likely to pay for their on-the-job education...the *expensive* way.

The set of documents, and the terms and conditions they include, are surprisingly unique to each deal. Negotiating purchase agreements is a complex legal process sprinkled with critical business decisions. While the subject is more extensive than we can address here, the following paragraphs provide a sampling of the topics that you may encounter in negotiating the Purchase & Sale Agreement and other documents.

Most fundamentally, your Purchase & Sale Agreement will establish the *structure of the transaction* by, at a minimum, specifying:

- Exactly what you are buying: the seller's stock or his assets
- Which assets and liabilities are included or excluded from the sale
- How much you will pay
- When and in what form you will pay the seller
- Whether you will make a Section 338(h)(10) election
- How the price will be allocated to asset classes for tax purposes
- Seller and buyer representations and warranties
- Terms and conditions for consulting agreements, covenants not-to-compete, and seller financing
- The seller's liability for built-in gains or cash-to-accrual taxes
- Escrows and holdbacks, how much cash will be retained in each, and how/when the cash will be distributed

In general, the transaction's structure includes actions that will happen for sure. However, the longest and most complex parts of the Purchase & Sale Agreement deal with protections and resolutions for things that may have occurred in the past, and things that may happen in the future.

In the Purchase & Sale Agreement, you and the seller will *represent* and *warrant* certain things to be true. The agreement also will specify *indemnifications*, mostly on the seller's side, for damages in case any of the representations or warranties are not true, an untoward event occurs, or an error in the seller's claims or financial records is discovered after closing. Sellers (often jointly and severally if there are more than one) are liable for the damages. Escrows, holdbacks, and offsets are set up so you (the buyer) can collect damages, if any, quickly and easily.

The agreement also sets a maximum, called *the cap*, on the seller's total liabilities. Depending on circumstances, the cap is usually 10 to 30 percent of purchase price for general representations and warranties. To avoid the seller being nickeled and dimed, the agreement may define a minimum claim size for liabilities and establish a bucket—typically 1 percent of the purchase price. The seller won't pay any claims until the total of all claims exceeds the bucket amount, at which time *the bucket tips,* and the seller, must pay all of the accumulated claims. However, some items (e.g., fraud, willful misconduct, unpaid taxes, government contract claims, environmental damage, and ongoing litigation) may be excluded from the cap and the seller will have a larger liability, usually capped at 100 percent of the purchase price.

But the seller's liabilities will not last forever; *survival periods* are defined in the purchase agreement. Normally, the survival period for most representations, warranties, and contingencies is one to three years. When the survival period expires, any funds left in the related escrows will be distributed to the seller. If your deal uses holdbacks instead of escrows, you will pay the holdbacks to the seller at that time. For some items (e.g., taxes, legal claims, and government contracts), the survival period is usually thirty to sixty days longer than the statute of limitations. In certain situations (e.g., environmental liabilities), the survival period can be indefinite. Interestingly, survival periods generally do not apply when the seller is a publicly-traded firm.

You may specify not-to-compete provisions in the Purchase & Sale Agreement or in a separate document, depending on their complexity. In either case, the document should state clearly:

- Who is subject to non-competes: only the seller, selected or all shareholders, and/or key employees
- Extent of non-compete restrictions by industry, region, and term
- Non-solicitation of a list of customers
- Non-solicitation and non-hire of employees past, present, or future
- Non-disclosure of methods, processes, and trade secrets
- Non-disparagement of the buyer and the seller's former company

To make them enforceable, customize not-to-compete restrictions to fit the proceeds the person will earn from the transaction. For example, you may choose to pay a retention incentive to employees who will remain with the company after closing. That expense may be paid by the seller, by you, or shared between the two of you. Payments for non-compete agreements should be made over the term of the covenant. This enables the buyer to stop payments if the seller violates the covenant, and forces the seller to either accept nonpayment or pay to dispute the buyer's claim. One warning though: Having too many people subject to not-to-compete restrictions can enable some to hold the transaction hostage.

If the seller is providing financing, the Purchase & Sale Agreement will specify the type and extent of collateral you will offer the seller. If you also are using a third-party lender to fund part of the purchase price, most lenders will require that the seller financing be subordinated, and they have required provisions relative to subordination. Therefore, your attorney will need to coordinate with your lender. In addition, it is good practice to include a provision in the seller note that allows you to offset loan payments in case of a subsequent breach of representations. Such a provision is often less controversial than an escrow or holdback. To protect both parties, any buyer reduction should be held in a separate escrow until the parties agree on the amount of the reduction.

There are many other topics that could be covered in your Purchase & Sale Agreement. For example, in cool M&A markets stock-for-stock deals are common. That is not necessarily an adverse development. For openers, it gives you more pricing flexibility because the seller will not pay capital gains taxes when they receive stock instead of cash. But it does make the purchase agreement more complex in terms of the representations and warranties that you must make as the buyer.

In any case, to successfully close a deal that will work for everyone, thorough win-win negotiations are essential. Appreciating each other's needs, finding ways to satisfy them, and documenting them in the Purchase & Sale Agreement is the fastest path to closing. Remember, ultimately you can't win unless the seller on the other side of the table feels like he has won too. Experienced M&A negotiators are adept at inserting win-win thinking into the tedious, intense, and sometimes confrontational discussions that produce a Purchase & Sale Agreement that both sides are willing to sign. Have confidence in your negotiator—but review the documents thoroughly before you sign them!

MISTAKE #47

IGNORING THE WORLD AROUND YOU

A lot can change when a deal takes a long time to close—almost all of it bad!

In spring of 2008, a developer attempted to buy a business that included choice pieces of partially developed land. He submitted an LOI that the buyer accepted and started due diligence. Negotiations dragged on for months as the real estate market softened. He and the seller were only a million dollars apart in price—about 5 percent of the deal. The seller insisted that property values would increase and stood firm. The deal never closed. During the next year the bottom fell out of the market, the seller defaulted on loan payments, and the bank foreclosed. Rotten luck? *Yes.* Predictable? Also *Yes.* The buyer dodged a bullet while the seller drowned in a bad economy, but both did not appropriately respect the changing economic conditions as they negotiated the deal.

Consider a second example. The buyer couldn't raise sufficient cash through conventional loans, so he arranged financing through the Small Business Administration (SBA), which offered to guarantee a loan large enough to complete the transaction. The deal also involved partial seller financing. At the time the SBA rule was that the seller could not be paid before the SBA loan was repaid. However, the buyer and seller agreed it was necessary for the success of the acquisition for the seller to remain an employee after the sale. However, near the end of the negotiations, the SBA implemented a new rule that limited employment agreements with sellers to a year or less. Without the ability to retain the seller's services, the transaction collapsed—but not before both parties incurred several thousand dollars in accounting and legal fees.

Need a third example? During due diligence, newspapers announced that one of the seller's key customers had been sold. Since the seller's forecasts projected flat sales from that customer, the buyer was not concerned and proceeded to close the deal at the price specified in the LOI. But two months after closing, revenue from the customer dropped by three-quarters, causing a 20 percent drop in overall profit. The buyer had no recourse because both parties were aware of the pending sale of the key customer, and the buyer did not insert a contingent adjustment in the purchase agreement to protect against a drop in revenue or profits.

Buyers should be keenly aware of changes in the business world that occur while the transaction is being negotiated. Mentally, buyers often become married to a deal and *"drink their own Kool-aid."* Among the popular flavors of buyer Kool-aid is the erroneous belief that they can manage the seller's business better and more profitably than the seller did. In the short term, that is rarely true.

Not every change that occurs in late-stage negotiations and just after closing is bad—just most of them.

Early in 2008, a buyer closed a deal to acquire a company that specialized in support for Army Special Forces. It was the peak of the market, and the buyer paid top dollar. But market demand for the services grew faster than the seller had projected. Furthermore, the buyer's and seller's staffs developed an extraordinary synergy that enabled them to rapidly expand existing contracts and win work with new customers. The acquisition outperformed by 20 percent the growth projected in the *pro forma* financials used to obtain Board of Directors' approval for the purchase. It was a fortunate acquisition all around: the right market, at the right time, with the right people—but neither the buyer nor the seller recognized the synergy during negotiations.

Most experts agree that buying a company typically takes five to nine months from the initial contact until closing, but the time frame varies widely. When the buyer has a proven search-and-screen process, and routinely collects information about potential target companies, the time frame is often shorter. However, when the seller's company hasn't been groomed to be sold or the seller has unrealistic price expectations, risks increase and the sale may drag on. Along with inflated seller valuations, the factor that most often delays closing is a lack of documentation such as: audited financial statements, revenue projections, clear title to assets and intellectual property, loan agreements, and questionable stock ownership and transfer records.

Market conditions can change dramatically in twelve months, but fewer changes happen in four months. Common external changes that can affect the M&A market and prices include:

- *Legislative & Regulatory Uncertainties,* such as in the health care and insurance industries when Congress was debating potential massive changes in the U.S. health care system.
- *Market Changes* like the dot-com crash, real estate crash, and rise in oil prices that influenced sales multiples positively or negatively.
- *Rule Changes* like capital gains tax laws and SBA guidelines that affect the net proceeds of a transaction.
- *Economic Shifts* like rising interest rates and shifting loan criteria that change buyers' ability to obtain affordable financing.

The key point is *close your deal as quickly as possible*, and look for changes in these four areas that may occur as you plan and execute your acquisition strategy.

A short word of caution: Buyers tend to make the worst deals in hot markets with vigorous competitive bidding for target companies. Who could forget the hottest market in history: the dot-com era from 1998 to 2000 when Internet companies with zero revenue raised tens (sometimes hundreds) of millions in equity dollars on the mere promise of a web-based business. Conversely, more favorable deals occur in cool markets when money is tight and demand is low—if you can afford a purchase.

In general, expect a flurry of M&A activity after any major economic shift like a large rise or fall in commodity prices (e.g., oil and steel), a technological breakthrough, deregulation, or a change in consumer demand (e.g., demographics). The bustle occurs because buyers see opportunity where sellers see risk and uncertainty. The bottom line is this: Don't pressure yourself into choosing a marginal target company because you set an unrealistic deadline. No transaction at all is better than a bad transaction. Keep searching for the ideal candidate no matter how long it takes—and be aware that market conditions will change dramatically over time. The old adage *"Buy low, sell high"* applies: best to buy in a down market and sell during a hyped-up market. But you already knew that, of course.

MISTAKE #48

DELAYING INTEGRATION PLANNING

Plan the integration during due diligence because, if you have difficulties integrating the seller's operations with yours, maybe you shouldn't buy his company.

A publicly-traded company who is a regular player in M&A markets plans the integration during due diligence to support the buy decision, to validate the price, to provide inputs to legal agreements, and to budget integration and operational costs. The specific approach to operational integration varies according to circumstances, of course, but one rule of thumb is they always keep the seller's organization intact when it is merged into their organization. They never split the seller's operations by sending part of it to one of their divisions, part to another division, and so forth.

To maintain the teamwork and synergy that enabled the seller's business to be successful, they either integrate it as whole in an existing division or operate it semi-autonomously. When the seller has a strong brand recognition, they let the seller's organization keep its name and their business cards read: *ABC Company—A Division of XYZ*. By doing integration planning during due diligence, they:

- Determine specific requirements to be documented in a consulting agreement with the prior owner
- Define duties, performance expectations, and items to be included in employment agreements with the seller's key managers
- Obtain material for use in post-closing briefings and meetings with the seller's former employees

These actions enable the merged operations to hit the ground running immediately after closing.

The deal doesn't end when you sign the check—it starts! The future success of the newly combined entity really depends on how well you integrate the seller's assets with yours. So due diligence should address integration questions rigorously to avoid nasty surprises and accelerate the shift from doing the deal to achieving the revenue and profit growth that you expect from the deal.

Until you know exactly how the seller's operations will merge with yours to produce higher revenue and profits, the price you are paying is based on unsubstantiated optimism. Therefore, we recommend that you prepare a written integration plan during due diligence. The plan should specify integration objectives to be achieved and tasks to be performed during the first ninety days after closing in the back office (e.g., human resources, accounting, legal, and facilities) and in the front office (e.g., business development and customer service). Involve the seller's key managers in the planning process by making integration strategies and approaches the focus of your due diligence interviews with them. If you can't see how the seller's business operations will merge with yours, you may want to reconsider buying the company in the first place.

One key question to resolve during due diligence is: *Do you need the previous owner to stick around and, if so, for what specific purpose and for how long?* Areas where you may require his help will emerge as you plan to integrate his customers, operations, and employees with yours. On the other hand, you have valid reasons for concern if the successful transition depends entirely on his presence. So verify that the seller's business offers products and services that have earned customer loyalty independent of relationships with the prior owner. Use answers from integration planning to develop an employment or consulting agreement for the seller, including the duration of the agreement and the specific tasks you want him to perform and goals you want him to accomplish.

Similarly, integration planning will reveal which employees are vital for customer retention and operational continuity. Consider requiring them to execute employment agreements as a condition of closing. Such agreements typically contain one-time bonuses, ongoing incentives, and non-solicitation covenants relative to customers and other employees. Performance metrics and goals established for the new organization are an excellent basis for the ongoing incentives. Interestingly, the current trend in M&A deals is to increase the number of employees required to sign employment agreements prior to closing.

Integration planning also should compare the processes, systems, and websites used by the two companies for e-mail, customer support, order processing, timekeeping, accounting, and the like. Identify the required process and system changes, their effect on staffing, and their hardware and software costs. Budget for these changes as if they were transaction costs because, in fact, they are. The transition plan should include an approach and a schedule for completing the changes, and assign a manager to direct their implementation.

Lastly, but by no means of least importance, is the matter of culture. Even if the target company looks perfect on paper, the integration and performance risk is increased if their culture doesn't mesh with yours. Cultural mismatch is a euphemism for differences in strategies, values, and attitudes. Such mismatches often materialize when you attempt to merge the two staffs and integrate business functions. When potential conflicts, personalities, or egos dictate your organizational or personnel assignment decisions, you may have a dangerous cultural mismatch. Likewise, when you and the seller have irreconcilable "right ways" of performing sales, customer service, or other functions, it is likely that you have a cultural mismatch. The best time to discover and resolve (if possible) such mismatches is during due diligence—long before you sign the purchase agreement and transfer the funds. If you don't take specific action to resolve such mismatches and proceed with the deal anyway, you may be buying yourself a major headache!

CHAPTER FIVE

INTEGRATION—GETTING THE PAYOFF

Poor integration planning ranks with overpayment and weak strategic fit as the top three reasons why acquisitions fail.

One of the most famous integration failures of all time began in 1998 when Daimler-Mercedes purchased Chrysler. Each company had a long history of success. Daimler-Mercedes was formed when Daimler and Benz merged in 1926. Known for world-class engineering, they produce Mercedes cars that have led the high-end market for decades. Chrysler, formed in 1925, builds well-engineered cars for middle-class Americans—it built the first minivans. On paper, it was a merger made in heaven that should have produced major advances in shared technologies, streamlined procurement, and complementary research and development (R&D) programs.

Instead, the merger initiated an ugly nine-year cultural battle. In addition to international competition and a slowing world economy, several internal factors combined to sabotage the merger. For example:

- *Cultural Mismatch:* The Germans felt the Americans were a weak sister that built cheap cars for the middle class. The Americans saw the Germans as brilliant and diligent, and expected them to stay in Germany. But, from day one, the Germans dominated the merger.

- *Pay Disparities:* The Germans felt the Americans were paid more to perform the same jobs. For example, Chrysler's CEO earned $11 million per year while his German counterpart was paid $2 million. Would the Americans cut their pay, or would the Germans receive a big pay hike? The issue was an elephant in the room at meetings.

- *Different Markets:* Mercedes' core buyers were luxury car owners who sought brand-name recognition, so they used a high-cost, low-volume business model. Chrysler, on the other hand, designed and built cars for buyers who were price sensitive and fuel-economy minded, so their business model was low-cost, high-volume.

- *Union Issues:* Workers in both companies were members of unions who jealously guarded their prerogatives and compensation, and were afraid that the merger would result in massive layoffs.
- *Barriers to Shared Technology:* Mercedes and Chrysler seemed to have complementary technologies in engines, transmissions, safety features, and passenger comforts. But mistrust and *"We're better than them"* attitudes blocked virtually every attempt to share their know-how.

The merger demonstrates how leadership conflicts, cultural mismatches, hostile labor, and mistrust can obliterate corporate strengths and destroy a merger. Damage from the failed integration was irreparable. In 2007, Daimler-Mercedes sold Chrysler to Cerberus, and just two years later, Chrysler accepted a federal bailout and declared bankruptcy.

Poor integration planning ranks with overpayment and weak strategic fit as the top three reasons why M&A deals fail to produce value for the buyer. In earlier chapters of this book, we looked at the business, legal, and financial aspects of a deal. Too often, executives focus on those aspects to the exclusion of intangible human issues—the social aspects of a deal such as leadership, culture, and communications.

Since human issues are difficult to manage, they are easy to ignore. Operational, legal, and financial issues can be diagnosed and resolved in straightforward ways. But executives know that people are the heart of any organization and resolving human issues is vital for success. More people means more human issues—so the complexity of integration escalates. The seven top challenges to be concerned about during integration include:

- Avoiding interpersonal conflicts that can sink even the best deal
- Aligning the management structure and agreeing on long-term goals
- Capitalizing on cross-selling opportunities and service/product delivery efficiencies as quickly as possible
- Defusing doubts about the merger among old and new employees
- Minimizing the inefficiency and costs of maintaining parallel processes and systems for an extended period

- Choosing best practices from each of the two companies and adopting them throughout the new entity
- Creating an exciting new culture that embraces everyone

Don't underestimate the importance of these challenges and the effort required to reach agreements and implement changes.

The manner in which you announce the purchase sets the tone for the entire integration process. You and the seller should coordinate how you reveal the sale because there is a pecking order for spreading the news and answering questions. First, use one-on-one meetings with the people who are vital to your success: large clients, strategic partners, and key employees. Continue with announcements to people whose support is also important to the business, and then make an announcement to your industry and the local community through media outlets.

In a perfect world, you would have planned integration in such detail during due diligence that the day after closing you can tell each person in your company and the seller's company:

- Their new position title and responsibilities
- Their boss's name and names of their direct reports
- Their office location and working hours
- Their salary, benefits, goals, and incentive plan
- Policy and procedure revisions for the merged organization
- How to log into the new intranet, e-mail, and accounting systems

In the real world, that is a tall order! So this chapter offers best practices for avoiding mistakes in blending the companies relative to:

- Organizational structure and people
- Marketing and sales processes
- Service and product delivery processes
- Contracting and accounting systems, processes, and staffing
- Facilities and computer systems
- Human resource practices, benefit programs, and culture

Performance measures and metrics are vital in each area because: *"What gets measured, gets done!"*

THE UNEMPLOYABLE ENTREPRENEUR

*If the former owner doesn't have a specific
and essential role in the transition, gently
push him out the door as soon as possible.*

A s required in the employment contract that was part of the Purchase & Sale Agreement, the buyer retained the seller as a full-time employee. The contract term was four years with the first two years' salary and a minimum bonus guaranteed. The company had the right to buy out the last two years of the contract for one year's salary. The seller's job was to cross-sell products and services to the buyer's customers and to his former customers. It never happened. The seller's personal performance fell far short of the mutually agreed upon goals, and revenue from his former customers atrophied considerably during the first year. The reason was that he spent more time defending his escrow accounts than selling and servicing customers. Because of the precipitous decline in revenue and other factors, he lost all of the escrows anyway.

A second seller became an employee of a publicly-traded company when the sale was closed. It was a small deal that didn't allow the seller to retire, so he really had no choice but to continue working. The sales agreement specified four equal cash payments, the first at closing and the remaining three at one-year intervals. Among other provisions, the agreement included a clause under which the seller would forfeit all of the remaining payments if his employment was terminated for cause. One termination-for-cause proviso said if the seller "*consistently failed to follow policies or procedures after being given written notice and a period to correct*," then the seller could be terminated. His primary post-sale responsibility was to gain new clients, since his former clients were serviced by the buyer's staff. But he didn't feel that the buyer's staff took adequate care of his former clients, so he frequently jumped in to resolve issues if they complained. When the economy took a nosedive and sales declined, the company claimed that the seller spent too much time with former clients, so they threatened (in writing) to invoke the termination clause. Needless to say, the relationship grew strained even though neither party was willing to risk ending it.

These two horror stories were a disaster for both the buyer and seller. The simple reason is that entrepreneurs are high-risk employees. Former business owners are frequently unemployable because they are used to operating independently. For years, they made the rules and told others what to do. So whatever the relationship is between you and the seller during negotiations, expect it to deteriorate after closing. For example, Dick acknowledges that it would have been extremely difficult for him to work in his former company after closing and take direction from the President and new owners.

When the seller has a vested interest in the success of the business, provisions for a continuing relationship after closing usually must be included in the sales agreement—but match the nature of the post-sale relationship to the nature of the vested interests. For example, the seller will be concerned about the company's future success if the seller:

- Receives earn-out payments that depend on performance
- Provides seller financing under terms of a promissory note
- Leases real estate and/or equipment to the company
- Receives continuing payments under a covenant not-to-compete or a consulting agreement
- Remains a contingent guarantor on company debt, or is a signatory on performance bonds or guarantees to trade creditors

In each case, the seller will want follow-up mechanisms to be specified in the sales agreement, but that doesn't necessarily mean that he should be an employee. Among the most common follow-up mechanisms are:

(1) Automatically receiving a copy of internally-prepared financial statements on a monthly or quarterly basis

(2) Automatically receiving a copy of the annual audit report

(3) Having the right to examine company records on request

(4) At his own expense, having a mutually-agreeable CPA review or audit the company's records and financial reports

If the previous owner must remain with the business for an extended period after closing, prepare him to accept the fact that the business is not his anymore. Remember, the seller is accustomed to being in charge—deciding what and how things should be done. It will be very easy for him to slip back into that role, and for former employees to treat him as they always have. To gracefully remove the seller from center stage, consider these tips to build your own personal relationships with customers and the staff:

- Occupy the seller's former office since the staff is used to going to that office to report results and get things approved
- Encourage the seller to take a *supporting* role in decision-making
- Request that the seller redirect questions from the staff to you rather than to answer them himself
- Use the seller as a source of advice and recommendations, but be sure that the staff comes to you for that purpose
- Request the seller to avoid saying "I recommend" or "I think the best choice is" when dealing with customers—use "we" instead
- Give the seller plenty of time off and encourage him to take vacations, especially in the first month after closing

Despite your best effort to cooperate with the former owner, the day will come when you will want to manage business without the seller around. The truth is, about the same time, the seller also may want to move on. Think of that day when you are drafting the consulting or employment agreement. You are obligated to meet the terms of those agreements unless you both agree to cancel them. We recommend that, except for unusual cases, you keep the former owner around for the shortest possible time!

LETTING KEY ASSETS WALK AWAY

In employee retention, relationships are more powerful than compensation—and that's even more true after an acquisition.

An executive with over twenty years in the personnel placement business reports that M&A transactions have produced some of the worst horror stories he has encountered in his career—and some of the most lucrative engagements. Executives, mid-level managers, scientists, engineers, and highly-qualified IT people have come to him to flee the wreckage of an acquisition. In his experience, there's one job-seeker from the buyer side for every three on the seller side. After seeing the common mistakes that companies make, he offered the following recommendations:

- *Plan Ahead.* When a sale is announced, the buyer's and the seller's employees want to know what will change and how it affects them. Plan the new organization, titles, roles, goals, and compensation in due diligence, and communicate them to the staff during the first week. Employees may leave if they don't know what is happening.
- *Hear Your New Employees.* Employees from an acquired company often feel as if they have lost their voice. They don't know who to talk to about ideas and concerns. Managers may feel like they have lost their standing, and have no say in new policies and procedures. Managers and employees may leave if nobody hears them.
- *Communicate, Communicate.* It may seem like a cliché, but a buyer can never communicate too much with employees after a sale. Use multiple media: meetings, newsletters, personal contact, and even broadcast e-mails. Reach out to old and new employees alike to tell them that they matter and are valued.
- *Involve Employees in Changes.* Form working groups to address specific

integration issues. An executive should articulate the new strategy, establish objectives for the group, and check in often to hear concerns and initiate action on the group's recommendations.

- *Keep the Best of Both Worlds.* Expect competition between the old and the new, particularly in marketing and sales. Look for effective practices from the acquired company and meld them with practices used in your company. Defuse us-versus-them bickering as quickly as possible.
- *Preserve Traditions.* Build morale by preserving traditions of both companies. For example, one acquired company was very proud of its volunteer service program. Employees as a group would donate services to a charity. Employees from the buyer were invited to join that group, which created connections among the employees.

None of these recommendations are particularly surprising, but very few buyers actually implement all six of them. We all know that employees vote with their feet. A sure sign that the acquisition may have problems is when your most valuable assets start to walk away from the company to look for jobs with one of your competitors.

Since people are a company's most precious resource, one focus of the integration effort must be to retain and merge human resources at all levels from the executive suite to the reception area. Employees are not interchangeable assets; instead, they are complex beings driven as much by emotion as by logic.

Unfortunately, some executives move employees around in their business as if they were pieces on a chessboard without even inquiring about their feelings, goals, or preferences. Of course, positions will be shuffled and lives will be disrupted during the integration that follows an acquisition. The disruptions are unavoidable. But if you are directing the changes, be sensitive to the personal issues and concerns of the employees whose lives you are disrupting.

You can create any kind of relationship you want with managers and employees from the company you just acquired. The relationships can be close or distant; friendly or formal; intra-dependent or independent; intimate or shallow; business, personal, or both. You won't have enough time to do everything you would like during integration, but allocating time to build relationships has to be a priority. Sometimes, all it takes is a minute to send a thinking-about-you e-mail.

As the buyer, you will want to retain the most competent executives, and put them in positions of authority. Ideally, the updated organization chart was designed during due diligence, and you are confident that it will work. If you have lingering doubts that the seller's key executives may resign after closing, maybe you should question the wisdom of the transaction. The new organization should be based on the go-forward strategy in order to increase the chances of:

- Achieving the first-year revenue and profitability goals
- Realizing synergies that motivated the transaction to start with
- Implementing better ways of doing business
- Getting the right managers in the right positions
- Knowing which managers to reassign or ask to leave

A strategy-oriented organization is more likely to put managers in jobs based on what they will achieve for the company, rather than what they may have done in the past, which company they came from, what titles they held, or how well they marketed themselves during due diligence—factors that all too often carry more weight than they deserve.

When retaining highly qualified employees at all levels is a concern, consider assigning an executive full time for four to six months to focus on retention. Your first line of defense against employee resignations is your reputation as an employer, substantiated by the personnel actions you take during the transition. Show the seller's employees and your own that future possibilities are bright individually and corporately.

If you didn't get them signed as a condition of closing, entice (maybe via a promotion or raise) key employees to sign an employment or non-compete agreement that restricts their ability to work for a competitor if they quit. Such agreements are common for executives, but they are being used increasingly for mid-level managers as well. The agreement may, for example, ban solicitation of customers, hiring of employees, or using proprietary information. However, in every case, the agreement must be reasonable and directly related to the employee's job duties.

Training programs and workshops are a great way to reassure old and new employees that their future is secure. Training forums can be useful in communicating the company's new strategy and priorities, and when personnel from both workforces are intermingled in a classroom, they will exchange experiences and get to know each other. Successful companies offer multiple training topics (e.g., product knowledge, customer background, skills development, and interpersonal relationships) to all staff levels in a variety of media such as online, classroom, off-site, and on-the-job.

Rarely in any acquisition are there productive jobs for everyone from both organizations. Furthermore, you may find during due diligence that some of the seller's employees are marginal performers (a few of your own employees may even fall into that category). For these two reasons, a clear picture of the new organization must be developed early to show why some people will stay while others must leave. This doesn't reflect on employees' intrinsic worth, only on their value to the new company.

With appropriate planning, you can hold the number of job losses to a minimum. In addition, proper implementation of the terminations can preserve corporate and personal dignity, and the right type of follow-up will preserve good will with departing employees. Compassionate and effective outplacement services provided by your human resources team or by an outplacement agency will make the best of a difficult situation.

Keep in mind that during the year following the acquisition, the new company's culture will be fragile, a living organism that is struggling to mature into its adult form. The more your employees and the seller's employees feel comfortable with each other and the emerging culture, the better. Internal community and company activities should be as easy as possible for all employees to join. In retention, relationships are more powerful than compensation—and that's even more true immediately after an acquisition.

MISTAKE #51

COMPENSATION QUAGMIRE

*Equalizing salary and benefits between old and new
employees is frequently a volatile post-closing issue.
Your solution must be sustainable in the long term.*

After carefully planning the integration and its financial implications
during due diligence, the buyer was ready for the explosive controversy
that occurred around salary and benefits after closing. The buyer's
salary structure was higher than the seller's, so the seller's employees lobbied
for salary increases. On the other hand, the seller's benefits were more generous, so the buyer's employees expected an upgrade in their benefit programs.
Having evaluated the problem from a competitive viewpoint, the buyer decided
to preserve its current compensation structure and was prepared to address the
fiery questions voiced by the seller's employees during briefings in the week
after closing—when the changes began to take effect. They compensated the
seller's employees for their newly reduced benefits through one-time salary
increases. For example, the seller had paid 100 percent of health care, so the
buyer upped the employees' salaries for the monthly premiums they would
pay as new participants in the buyer's health plan.

In another acquisition, the seller rewarded its top performers with an annual
"Achiever's Trip" to the Caribbean or Europe. To ameliorate the employees'
disappointment over losing that benefit, the buyer agreed to offer the trip at
the end of the first year as a special "reunion cruise" for all seller employees
who stayed with the company. In addition, most of the seller's long-tenured
employees were entitled to eight weeks annual leave, much higher than the
buyer's most generous leave. As a retention mechanism, the buyer agreed to
grandfather this leave entitlement for the employees. The financial effect of
these concessions was recognized in the closing price. For the most part, since
the seller gave the benefits prior to the sale, their effect on profitability was
already reflected in the seller's income statement.

Compensation is frequently a post-closing issue, and any concessions granted to the seller's employees should be economically sustainable in the long term. Expect and prepare for myriad questions from the seller's employees immediately after closing:

- Will I keep my job, and if so, will I get a raise or a bonus?
- If I lose my job, what severance package will I get?
- Will I receive my annual bonus and profit-sharing this year?
- Will I be forced to change my family's health care coverage?
- Will my retirement benefits change?

These are risky questions relative to retention and morale. At the same time, the buyer's compensation experts must consider these questions from the company's broader financial perspective:

- Will we downsize and/or reassign employees?
- If we lay off employees, what severance package will we offer?
- Should we use an outplacement service?
- How will we equalize pay between their people and ours?
- What metrics will we use to measure and reward performance?
- Will we combine the two bonus and incentive plans?
- Will we combine our health plan and retirement plan? If so, how?
- What strategic, financial, and legal issues must we consider?

It is best to address these knotty questions during due diligence so that the answers can be implemented expeditiously after closing.

You actually have multiple degrees of freedom available to integrate the two compensation plans or to design a new one. For example, there are four categories of pay:

- *Base Pay* (also called salary) is a fixed amount that is usually paid weekly, bi-weekly, or monthly, and adjusted annually. Base pay is the largest part of compensation for most people, but for senior executives it can be half or less of total compensation.
- *Special Pay* includes geographical cost-of-living allowances, shift differentials, piece work, etc.
- *Bonus Pay* is a lump sum typically paid annually to employees for their past performance. Bonus amounts are often determined by management based on subjective criteria.

- *Incentive Pay* is variable compensation usually paid on an annual basis to selected employees if they meet pre-specified individual, team, and/or company goals. The incentives can be paid in cash or stock (either grants or options) and may not be paid at all if the minimum goal is not met.

In addition, there are several compensation mechanisms that commonly are implemented during or shortly after an acquisition:

- *Retention Bonuses* are payments made to specified employees if they remain with the company for a stated period after closing.
- *Non-Compete Bonuses* are payments made to key employees in return for them agreeing (in writing) not to compete with the company if they leave.
- *Signing Bonuses* are paid to managers who sign an employment agreement that usually contains not-to-compete provisions.
- *Severance Agreements* are payments to an employee in the event of a layoff by the company or in a subsequent change of control.

Taken together, the pay categories and compensation mechanisms offer substantial flexibility to merge compensation plans.

It's probably necessary to merge compensation plans if the company you acquired will be otherwise integrated with yours. However, in some cases, compensation integration is not necessary and actually could be detrimental. For example, financial acquirers usually maintain separate pay plans. And even in a strategic acquisition where other elements are fully integrated, it may still be appropriate to leave the seller's pay plan untouched if the company operates in a different industry or region since compensation differs so widely from industry to industry and region to region for similar positions.

Similarly, mature industries generally have higher salaries and lower variable pay (i.e., bonuses and incentives) than companies in early stage industries where variable pay is linked to market share, revenue growth, and product development. Compensation plans are especially difficult to align after a merger between a company with a lucrative incentive plan and a company with none. The bottom line is, as the acquirer, you get to decide the competitive nature of your compensation plan including: (1) the split between base pay and incentive pay; (2) whether base pay will be below market, at market, or above market; and (3) what benefits will be offered. Choose wisely to retain your key people.

MISTAKE #52

THROWING AWAY
SOMETHING SPECIAL

*Use every measure you can to embrace the seller's employees
and practices in your corporate family as quickly as possible.*

A serial acquirer had a custom of choosing something special about each acquired company's business practices and making it the standard way of doing business in his company. They publicized the new practice broadly, and recognized and rewarded responsible managers from the acquired company. For example, after one acquisition they adopted the employee training program and management software from the seller's company, and touted it as "industry's best practice." Employees from the acquired company trained employees from the old company in the new practices. This enabled them to meet employees throughout the company, and gave all of the employees from the acquired company an identity and a sense of contributing. In your integration, pick something from the acquired company to implement in your company: a marketing or production process, a human resources practice, or a financial process. It doesn't matter as long as the acquired company's employees knew and were proud of it, and it increases their sense of belonging.

Another serial acquirer had a proven approach to restore employee productivity after the sale. Immediately after the closing, the seller's CEO would announce the sale via e-mail. An hour later, the buyer's CEO sent a welcome-aboard e-mail inviting everyone to an all-hands meeting the following day. If the acquired company had several sites, simultaneous all-hands meetings were held on each site. At the all-hands meetings, an executive welcomed the acquired employees and HR people distributed a personalized package to each one. The package included an offer letter that outlined the employee's title, duties, salary, incentives, and benefits—obviously prepared during due diligence. It also had an employment application to be completed; an employment agreement to be signed; and a form to acknowledge receipt of the company's Policies & Procedures Manual, its Code of Conduct, and its rules for using IT systems. The HR staff was available after the all-hands meeting to receive the applications and signed forms, answer questions, and resolve issues. This approach helped the acquired employees regain their productivity on the second day with most of their questions answered—and that's about as good as you'll be able to do in your acquisition!

A large, publicly-traded company usually acquired small, privately-held companies, which simplified the integration process. Being subject to Sarbanes-Oxley, however, the CEO and CFO were required to certify quarterly financial results. So their top integration concerns included accurate accounting, closing the books on time, and extending internal controls to the acquired company. As a buyer, their normal practice was to integrate the seller's company into their accounting, timekeeping, invoicing, and human resource (e.g., payroll, health plan, and retirement plan) processes. As added protection to ensure the accounting transfer met Wall Street's tight reporting timetable, closing was scheduled ten days after the agreements were signed (thirty days if the Hart-Scott-Rodino Act applied). During that interim period, they processed timesheets and prepared billings using everyone in the seller's accounting department for sixty days. In the long run, however, they kept about one-third of the seller's accounting staff, more if their accounting department was short-staffed or if the seller's business required special expertise.

In another case, the acquirer was very disappointed with sales results of the acquired company during the first six months after closing, and decided to make dramatic changes in the sales force. They replaced two of the seller's most experienced and highest paid salesmen. Regrettably, the acquirer had failed to review and understand the sales cycle of the acquired company during due diligence, which clearly showed that the acquired company usually generated a majority of its sales in the second half of the calendar year. Since the acquisition closed in December, the so-called "disappointing" sales results were roughly the same as recent years. If the buyer had been aware of the company's annual financial cycle, they might not have replaced the best salesmen. Unfortunately, it took several years for sales to recover from the buyer's rash actions.

Extending your financial controls into the acquired company must be a top priority after an acquisition. Ideally, your controls are state-of-the-art, but if not, integration is an excellent opportunity to improve them across the entire company. Internal controls include a management process, overseen by senior executives and the Board of Directors, that provides reasonable assurances that the company's:

- Operations are effective and efficient
- Financial reporting is accurate, complete, and timely
- Activities comply with applicable laws and regulations

Internal controls have five interrelated elements: cyclical monitoring activities, regular performance measurements, candid risk assessments, timely information distribution, and open communication channels.

Be prepared to hit the ground running with respect to imposing your internal controls on the acquired company. Among the basics of internal controls, one that should receive immediate attention on day one is cash management: Take control over all cash receipts and disbursements from the acquired company on the day the acquisition closes. Best practice is to open a new checking account and have all receipts deposited into that account(s). Limit access to the new account(s) to designated employees. A second best practice is to establish separate accounts for payroll and accounts payable with designated signatory levels on checks. Integrating the acquired company into your budgeting process is another area that deserves prompt attention.

Time is of the essence in an effective integration. The longer that integration takes, the higher the risk it will fail. Among the top reasons why integrations fail is that the buyer wasn't aware of and didn't satisfy the financial needs and concerns of the acquired employees—not always an easy thing to do. The experts we interviewed agree that expeditious integration is the key to success, especially when the acquired company operates in a different geographical region than the buyer. They say sixty days from closing (certainly less than a calendar quarter) is a reasonable time period to complete financial and employee integration.

MISTAKE #53

MIXING OIL AND WATER

*If cultural differences aren't addressed and resolved
shortly after closing, your return-on-investment
for the acquisition may be a major disappointment.*

Before beginning his own company, Dick was a group manager with a consulting firm that was bought by the IT division of a large aerospace company. The integration was a cultural catastrophe from day one. The median age in the consulting firm was mid-thirties (Dick was thirty-six). But when Dick visited headquarters for business development meetings with peers from other parts of the aerospace company, he was among the youngest people in the meeting. He was a young buck trying to fit in a network of fifty-something "good ol' boys." Obviously, it would be ten years or more before he could become a Vice President; he was just plain too young. Dick was accustomed to promotions based on results, but it seemed like age and social connections were valued more highly in the culture of the aerospace company. Because of those cultural differences, it's not at all surprising that the acquisition failed to yield the anticipated cross-selling opportunities and revenue growth.

In another acquisition, a conservative, 100-year-old bank was bought by a comparatively young, risk-taking, fast-growing bank. The culture of the old bank was to cultivate personal relationships with customers, many of whom had been clients of the bank for several generations. On the other hand, the growth strategy of the young bank was to offer new services, embrace new technologies, and operate more efficiently. Both cultures were innovative and effective, but one grew by incrementally improving its methods and rewarding relationships, while the other focused on inventing new things and rewarding new ideas. As you might guess, the post-merger culture shock was stressful, the integration took a year longer than planned, and it was only completed following a large staff turnover.

Most integration issues originate directly or indirectly from a lack of sensitivity to cultural differences. Prior to the acquisition, the buyer and seller each operated in a distinct culture that included ethics, a business philosophy, a dress code, ways to resolve issues, and other generally accepted standards and behaviors. When two cultures are incongruous, integration is like mixing oil and water. Workplace diversity further complicates integration. We usually consider diversity to be an advantageous trait because it stimulates innovation and out-of-the-box thinking. However, diversity also can be the source of irreconcilable disagreements. In an integration where there are ego clashes and people are pushed into uncomfortable positions, valuable employees may quit.

The potential for cultural clashes that erode morale is one of the most important, but often overlooked, issues in planning integration. Since companies are groups of people, human factors are vital to the success of the integration and, ultimately, the acquisition. Expecting revenue to increase when merging companies with different beliefs, values, and work styles is a big risk. Which of the two cultures will prevail in the new organization, and how will that culture impact the productivity of employees in the company whose culture has been discarded?

Corporate culture has a hierarchy that must be considered in merging employees, processes, and systems from two companies:
- Shared beliefs and assumptions that are
  - Created or adopted by managers and employees as they
    - Wrestle with the opportunities and challenges of
      - Adapting to external and internal changes in ways that
        - Have worked in the past and will work again, and
          - Can be taught to new employees as the
            - "Right way" to approach and resolve issues.
Employees in one company will interact with the employees in the other company according to this hierarchy in developing new relationships and a potential new culture. Where characteristics of the two companies are similar, those characteristics naturally will persist in the new culture. Where the characteristics are different, characteristics from the stronger company (usually the larger of the two) will triumph.

Quite often, a new culture begins to emerge during due diligence and negotiations as the parties work out terms of the agreement and resolve issues. Hostile or distrustful confrontations in due diligence can produce persistent suspicions and antagonism between the buyer's management team and the seller's team. Such negative feelings would be exacerbated by post-closing disagreements or litigation relative to the Purchase & Sale Agreement. Therefore, personalities of the accountants, attorneys, and consultants involved in due diligence and negotiations should be considered carefully from the cultural perspective.

You might ask: *Is it even possible to integrate companies that have substantial cultural differences?* The answer is *yes*, but success depends on recognizing and addressing the differences during due diligence and negotiations. In addition, employees need to be told soon after closing why the acquisition took place, how the two companies fit together, and what the new goals are. They also need to know how the culture of the combined company will differ from the culture they came from. When the culture differences are severe, it may be appropriate not to merge the workforces; instead allow them to operate independently. On the other hand, sometimes it may be wise to pull the plug on the acquisition before closing if cultural differences threaten post-closing success.

In most cases, employees don't know their culture's weaknesses and strengths or how they affect daily activities. Therefore, the integration program should follow four steps with respect to culture:

1) Include cultural compatibility in the *go, no-go* decision for a deal
2) Acknowledge that both company cultures are valid
3) Explain that it's not practical to maintain separate cultures
4) Combine cultures in a way that prevents the deal from exploding

These are easier said than done. However, if cultural differences are not addressed and resolved, you could be very disappointed in the return-on-investment you realize from the acquisition.

MISTAKE #54

OVERLOOKING THE SYNERGY

If you don't search for it, you probably won't find the synergy you hoped for when you made the acquisition.

D uring due diligence, the buyer spent considerable time evaluating the seller's organic growth strategy, business development methods, and pipeline opportunities. The seller's business development program was disciplined and well-managed, but there were holes. The Vice President who directed operational due diligence jokingly said to the seller's Vice President of Sales: "*Your pipeline is like ours—aces and spaces.*" The Seller's Vice President responded: "*Let's make it our priority when we close the deal. I think there are lots of ways to fill each other's holes.*"

That's exactly what they did. They formed a joint tiger team with six employees from each company. The tiger team's charter was to:

- Unify the companies' two organic growth plans
- Establish a common pipeline management methodology
- Identify cross-selling opportunities in the combined customer base
- Recommend sales and revenue goals, and an incentive plan
- Merge the two software development staffs, processes, and tools
- Integrate error reporting, change control, and version distribution
- Select best practices for service delivery and customer support
- Integrate the staffs, and standardize position descriptions and titles

It was a huge assignment for a small team, but the members had been hand-picked by their CEOs based on their personalities and knowledge of their company's operations. The group met in an off-site location for a full week starting the first Monday after closing.

Members of the tiger team met periodically during the following year to refine their plans and resolve issues. As you might expect, the results were extraordinary. Sales, revenue, and profit numbers all exceeded the buyer's expectations for the first year, within three months the two staffs operated as an integrated team, and no key employees were lost.

A second buyer wasn't as productive with his integration approach. Each of the buyer's managers was assigned to work with one or more counterparts in the seller's organization to unify processes and identify shared opportunities. When the conversations occurred at all, they were via phone or teleconferencing. Each pair of managers was supposed to make a joint progress report monthly, but no one followed up to ensure action was taken relative to the reports. The results of this approach also were as you would expect: A year after closing, the two companies were operating separately and there was little synergy.

The term *"under new management,"* whether it appears on the front page of the *Wall Street Journal* to proclaim a billion-dollar acquisition or in an e-mail to reveal the purchase of a small insurance agency, raises more fears than hopes in employees, customers, and suppliers. So what is the best way to ensure your acquisition will be seen as good news by everyone, including yourself? In our experience, a *tiger team* approach like that described in the first story works best because it:

- Gives both staffs an active voice in what happens
- Finds synergies that otherwise probably would go unnoticed
- Creates brand new opportunities
- Enables the new company to be a good supplier to its customers and a good customer to its suppliers

The tiger team approach promotes commitment, communications, and continuity among the two employee groups who are now one.

The military services originated the tiger team concept to produce quick results. A tiger team is a small, hand-picked, particularly skilled and capable group of "tigers" selected and chartered by a senior officer to plan and conduct a specific mission. Similarly, a business tiger team must include all the skills required to accomplish objectives for sales, marketing, engineering, operations, customer service, finance, legal, etc. Using tiger teams during integration has become an M&A best practice. Keep in mind that the integration of two large companies may require several tiger teams.

Tiger teams usually have equal representation from both companies so they can exploit history—a team dominated by one company is likely to perpetuate that company's history. Executives should designate tiger team members based on their open-mindedness, innovation, listening skills, and knowledge of how their company has operated in the past. The joint team will use history to chart future applications of the staffs and resources of both companies. Innovative new strategies, processes, and systems that boost sales, promote cross-selling, and cut costs frequently emerge from such unified think tanks.

Tiger teams often find synergies by putting the pieces together. For example, six ingredients are required for sustained growth in a market:

1) High-demand service and product offerings
2) Marketing materials and reference accounts
3) Relationships with customer executives and buyers
4) Relationships with technically-qualified strategic partners
5) Active contract vehicles with target customers
6) Staff members with technical credentials and training

Sometimes, one company may have several of these six, while the other company has the missing pieces essential for boosting sales.

At the end of the day, of course, implementation excellence is what determines the success or failure of an acquisition for both service and manufacturing firms. Tiger teams improve implementation of the new strategy by: (1) bringing knowledge of the other company's production and service delivery capabilities into their daily operations, (2) knowing who in the other company to contact to get answers, and (3) identifying training and investments required to merge systems and processes.

Buyers are frequently frustrated by the gap between their goals for an acquisition and what it actually achieves. They talk about synergy, but it doesn't happen until possibilities are converted into results. Without effective execution, integration actions may not be completed, deadlines may pass unnoticed, and stretch goals may shrink—all of which leave a buyer in worse shape than if the acquisition had never been attempted in the first place. Successful mergers require effective execution, and that is where tiger teams excel. Tiger teams can be the missing link between your goals for an acquisition and your end results.

MISTAKE #55

ONE YEAR LATER

Establish clear integration milestones and realistic performance goals to meet in the first year (or sooner).

After having minimal involvement with his former company during the year after closing, Dick met with the President in the company's office. The main subject of the meeting (liquidation of escrows) was resolved quickly, and the conversation shifted to the company's performance since closing. Seeming a bit frustrated and apologetic, the President reported that revenue had grown 15 percent, but profits were down. When Dick asked about the results he had expected, the President responded: "*This was as simple as a post-closing integration could be. You left, but the rest of the management team continued in their existing positions. I thought we would easily beat the annual goals we set before the sale.*" As far as Dick knew, there was no written integration plan.

The President had underestimated the extensive disruptions caused by any sale. Yes, the contracts, facilities, operating staff, and business development process were the same as before. But high-level executive responsibilities had been realigned (e.g., the former CEO was gone), and the management team was reacting to a different set of questions, ideas, and business priorities from new owners and a new Board of Directors. Furthermore, the venture capital firm had inserted a new CFO who changed basic accounting procedures, and the company had changed its working hours and implemented a new benefit structure. Those changes had revised the business model and significantly affected hourly rates and profitability.

A functional hole is usually created when a member of the seller's management team leaves the company after closing, especially roles that the former business owner played in the organization. What functions did the owner and other managers perform? Obviously, such functions are holes that must be filled during integration. If those holes cannot be filled by the buyer's management team or in other ways, then consider offering a consulting agreement to the departing owner and managers for a short period after closing.

A financial buyer's objectives in integration are very different from a strategic buyer's objectives. Their sole purpose is to grow the company for eventual resale, much as one would buy and hold a stock. They have no intentions of integrating the operations, resources, or systems of the acquired company with their own company like a strategic buyer would normally do. Financial buyers (in Dick's case, the buyer was a venture capital firm) do not directly manage the company they acquire. Rather they control and monitor ongoing operations through aggressive growth and profitability goals, financial restructuring, and very close oversight mechanisms.

Any way you look at it, an acquisition is a jolt to normal operations— plan on it! Schedule integration activities to be completed in a year or less by establishing specific tasks and milestones in each integration area: sales, operations, research and development (R&D), information systems, and back office functions. Employees in both companies should be expected to work together to make changes happen beginning the day after closing. That's why it is crucial to document integration objectives, milestones, and activities during due diligence—after closing is the time to execute the plan. In addition, establish measures of success and set achievable performance goals in each area. If possible, implement clear incentives for achieving the milestones and meeting the goals.

Integration is especially problematic for people who think that details will take care of themselves. That is a dangerous attitude in every aspect of an M&A transaction. For sure, attention to detail is important during negotiations, but not paying attention to detail during integration also can be fatal. The most effective integration efforts evaluate and plan for issues related to merging the two firms' cultural expectations, business processes, management teams, operating staffs, compensation programs, and information systems. The deals most likely to fail leave those details to chance.

MISTAKE #56

THE WORST THAT CAN HAPPEN

To avoid a failed integration, prepare a thorough integration plan during due diligence AND manage its execution closely.

A group of entrepreneurs with financial and legal backgrounds began a roll-up in construction materials. In just two years, they acquired three companies with a total of $25 million in annual revenue. The companies were family-owned organizations with virtually no formal infrastructure such as a management team, automated business systems, or progressive supplier and distribution relationships. By cross-selling and streamlining management, they were able to increase sales organically to $35 million in the 2005–2007 peak construction period.

Their plan was to build a $100 million company on the east coast and then flip it. They bought new equipment and rolling stock, opened two distribution centers, and built computer systems from scratch to manage their production and financial operations—all financed with debt. They hired a President to integrate and manage the business since the owner-managers of the acquired companies left after their respective closings. But after two years, he was fired for cause. As if that wasn't enough, the economic downturn hit the construction industry. Sales dropped sharply, cash flow was too little to carry the debt load, and they filed for Chapter 11 bankruptcy. That's the worst that can happen—a truly unsuccessful integration. This integration crashed and burned for three reasons: (1) the operational infrastructure was put in place *after* the acquisitions, (2) a management structure was built *after* the acquisitions, and (3) capital was inadequate to finance post-closing infrastructure investments. All three of those "mistakes" were discussed in Chapter 2.

Bank mergers are notorious for awkward integrations—a model *not* to follow! For example, in a town near Stuart's and Dick's homes, you can stand at the door of a branch of the seller's bank and look across the road to see a branch of the buyer's bank. What's more, branch offices of two other banks are on the other corners of the intersection. It was clear to customers and employees alike that one of the two offices must close. But which one? What would happen to the two bank staffs? How would the ATM and other systems change? Would customers be satisfied with the new processes and services they would receive after the operational merger? Nearly two years later, one of the branch offices finally closed. But not before there was a 50 percent turnover in staff, and almost a 20 percent drop the combined customer base. That's the second worst thing that can happen in an integration gone awry: high operating costs, losing customers, and losing key employees. In this case, the integration failed to deliver the anticipated return-on-investment because of lack of a clear plan for post-closing integration actions, and what appeared to be a lack of management decisions and daily oversight of the integration process.

Many buyers expect cost savings from the integration to partially offset the acquisition price and produce value from the transaction. If that's the case for you, set a cost savings goal in the integration plan, identify baseline costs, and specify mechanisms for tracing actual cost savings. Time is of the essence for recovering savings during integration. Unless savings are realized within a reasonable time after closing, integration fatigue can set in and diminish the possibility of finding further savings. A rule of thumb is that the buyer can expect to find 4 to 6 percent in operational savings within twelve months after closing an acquisition. For example, if the purchase price is $20 million, the buyer can expect and look for about $1 million in cost reductions in the first year from personnel reductions, process improvements, facility consolidations, and the like.

Delays in vital personnel decisions, process improvements, facility closings, and system consolidations usually indicate there never was an integration plan, or it is being poorly managed. Similarly, a narrow view relative to reducing operating costs can result in laying off employees who are essential for a successful integration. As a result, valuable time can be lost and needless operating costs incurred. On the other hand, an effective manager can often be the key player who makes an integration work. Effective execution of and management involvement in the integration plan is required to avoid the worst that can happen!

MISTAKE #57

MAKING NEW LEGENDS

Integration is complete when managers and employees in the merged organization no longer remember which company they came from.

L ockheed-Martin Corporation, the world's largest defense contractor by revenue, began operations in 1995 after the merger of the Lockheed Company with the Martin-Marietta Company. Both companies had long and proud traditions. The Lockheed Company, founded in 1916, was known for building the *U-2* and *Blackbird* spy planes and the *Polaris* and *Trident* submarine-launched missiles; whereas, the Martin-Marietta Company, with roots back to 1907, was famous for manufacturing the *Viking* moon-lander and space shuttle components.

Today the company has about 150,000 employees, and even the old-timers have forgotten that years ago they worked for one or the other of the two companies. Lockheed-Martin is making new legends including the F-35 *Lightning* and the F-22 *Raptor* (the world's most advanced jet fighters), missile and space systems, and secure computer systems. An integration is complete when the employees in the merged company no longer care about or even remember which company they came from.

If you've been through an acquisition as an executive or an employee on the seller side, you probably remember the doubts and questions you felt after the sale. Recall your early interactions with new co-workers from the buyer's organization. What messages did you get from them? What legends did they tell you about? Who were the heroes in those legends, and what did they do to achieve that status? What behaviors were judged as acceptable and unaccept-able? Those messages, legends, heroes, and behaviors were the culture of the buyer's company by whom you were now employed. You brought messages, legends, heroes, and behaviors from the culture of your former company too, but somehow they are generally less important than the buyer's culture.

Now that you are on the buying side, use those experiences to shape the current integration. The seller's managers and your own managers go into the integration with different goals and concerns, so an effective integration must satisfy the needs of both of the management teams. For example, the seller's managers usually are concerned that:

- They may have less authority and status in the new organization
- They may have to learn new jobs, processes, and tools
- Their compensation may be cut

And that assumes they aren't worried about losing their jobs to start with. Conversely, your managers are probably concerned about maintaining their authority and delivering the results that are expected of them—the results you used to justify the deal. The buyer's managers should feel obligated to produce the new customers, increased profits, streamlined supply chain, and other payoffs that were projected for the acquisition.

Therefore, the goal of the integration is to unify the two management teams behind a shared purpose. Managers from the two companies will either: (1) support the merged company's new purpose, (2) reject that purpose and leave, or (3) in rare cases, motivate the company to shift its purpose. Most managers will accept the new purpose if it enables them to achieve their professional goals in context with the company's goals.

Human beings believe in a purpose because of their experiences, not because of a training lecture or an employee manual. Any inconsistency between their post-closing experiences and the company's new purpose will undermine growth of the new culture. So, to monitor the cultural progress of the integration, ask key managers to describe the company's purpose and their experiences. If they don't answer instantaneously and consistently, you probably need to create new legends that demonstrate the company's new purpose and goals.

Your integration is complete when no one on either side remembers that there used to be two companies. For example, most employees of Northrop-Grumman and Lockheed-Martin don't remember that there once were two separate companies, even though the company's name on their business cards is a constant reminder of that birthright.

MAKING NEW MISTAKES

*M&A markets shift like a pendulum from favoring
buyers to favoring sellers. That's why it is vital to be ready
to make an acquisition or to sell your company at any time.*

Y ou've just read about 57 mistakes—be brilliant and don't let them happen in your next M&A deal. We'd like to say that those 57 mistakes cover the entire spectrum of possible blunders, but they don't. We see creative gaffes and variants of the 57 mistakes in essentially every new deal. It's possible for you to make other mistakes even as you avoid the ones that are described in this book. So, in addition to providing you with a broad perspective on M&A processes and potential pitfalls, we hope this book also has cultivated your M&A intuition and helped you to *feel* what M&A transactions will be like.

Nearly a quarter of the mistakes we've told you about were directly related to building and eventually selling Dick's company. He admits that selling the company he founded and grew for twenty-two years was enlightening. He felt like he had prepared thoroughly for the transaction, but he wasn't ready either technically or psychologically.

It's been several years since Dick's deal closed. As he looks back, he claims to have done many things right—and they paid off handsomely. He assembled a seasoned management team; systematically removed financial warts; built an attractive book of business; developed credible projections of future sales, revenue, and cash flow; and retained a savvy group of advisors to guide him through the arduous eight months from offering his company on the market to closing the deal.

If he were to do it over again, one thing he says that he would change is his expectations about selling a business. He would have been better prepared to deal with the roller coaster of virtually daily breakthroughs and breakdowns. Negotiating an M&A transaction requires sober assessments of the situation, candor with shareholders and executives about threats and opportunities, emotional and intellectual discipline in evaluating the alternatives, and the wisdom to *expect the unexpected*. For example, in three of the four months during due diligence, the company's revenue and profit fell well short of forecast, which gave the buyer negotiation ammunition to threaten to reduce the purchase price. On the other hand, the company won a three-year contract with a new government agency when it was a long shot in the competition. He also would have liked to have a better understanding about technical things like representations, escrows, and net asset value.

Dick also wishes he had started earlier to prepare for the transaction. Even though he felt the company was ready for the deal, several changes could have increased the company's value if they had been further along at the time of the sale. For starters, the company's capabilities could have been aligned more closely with the evolving priorities of customers and conditions in the M&A market. The company also should have invested more heavily in growth, probably by expanding the sales force. Those two changes alone could have added millions to the sales price—if only he had started a year or two sooner.

Current market conditions will be a major factor when it comes time for you to make a decision to buy a company or to sell yours. It was a seller's market when Dick sold his company in 2006: Credit was loose and multiple types of buyers were chasing deals. When this book was published in 2010, things had shifted to a buyer's market: Credit for M&A deals had dried up and only a few firms had the financial wherewithal to make acquisitions from current reserves. Firms who had cash (and were willing to spend it) could afford to be discriminating in their acquisition choices, and they could virtually dictate the terms of a deal. But M&A markets are like a pendulum—they shift back and forth from favoring the buyer to favoring the seller. Merger-mania comes and goes on a cyclical basis.

Despite dramatic shifts in the M&A markets and tax policies that can bewilder even the most experienced buyers and sellers, the future for M&A transactions is fairly predictable. Financial and strategic investors with capital and creative strategies will always be able to find first-rate opportunities at favorable prices. Likewise, businesses with profitable operations in growth fields (cyber-security, health care, intelligence, law enforcement, information technology, and logistics to name just a few) can attract buyers who may be willing to pay high multiples even in the worst of times. That's why it is essential to be prepared to pursue an acquisition or to sell your company when the market turns in your favor and presents an opportunity to achieve your goals.

If you are thinking about selling your business and you have read this far into this book, you know that your business is not the most important item on your agenda—you are. It's about you! Your business is not your life, although it makes a significant contribution to your life. Before you can sell your company, you must ask yourself and your significant other several questions: *What do I value? What lifestyle do I want? Who do I want to become?* When you arrive at the answers, you will know when to proceed with the sale. This book will help with the how-to.

Even if you're a buyer today, you need an exit strategy because some day you'll be a seller—and it might come sooner than you think. Failing to plan for the future can be an expensive mistake. If you are like most business owners, your business is your most valuable investment, and an exit plan is a crucial part of any effective investment strategy. Too many business owners get sucked into the day-to-day mechanics of running a business and lose sight of their future. So when it comes time to sell the company or transition ownership to an internal successor or a family member, they find themselves with few options. Most business owners don't realize that it takes two years (or longer) to sell and exit from their company.

We recommend that those among you who are (or intend to be) serial acquirers keep an Acquisitions Logbook. Make entries in the logbook on a daily basis as events unfold, and use it to keep the acquisition team and other executives informed about progress on the current acquisition. Logbook entries should cover the search for a target, LOI negotiations, due diligence, closing, and post-closing integration. Such a logbook is useful as a source of lessons learned for future acquisitions. Those of you who are making (or planning to make) your first acquisition can consider this book as the beginning of your Acquisitions Logbook.

Serial acquirers will benefit greatly from a feedback loop that records objectives, surprising events, actual results, and recommendations from each acquisition and external sources as a best practices repository for planning and managing the next acquisition and integration. Measures of performance to improve decision-making during future acquisitions are the cornerstone of such a feedback loop. This obvious step is often overlooked as serial acquirers measure the success of each acquisition on an *ad hoc* basis, often changing strategic goals and performance measures from one acquisition to the next. Instead, the measures and goals should be stable for a specific company and industry, and they should address market, financial, operational, and human resource factors.

In closing, we'd like to say one more time that we recommend you always be prepared to sell your company or to buy another company because such opportunities will arise when you least expect them. Furthermore, the actions you take to prepare your business to get maximum value from an M&A transaction are precisely the actions that will accelerate your company's growth and increase its profitability. Our wish is that all of your M&A transactions meet all of your expectations! We hope this book helps you achieve that goal.

APPENDIX

17 FACTORS THAT DETERMINE VALUE FROM THE BUYER'S PERSPECTIVE

Many buyers use a variation of the 17 factors listed in this Appendix to evaluate the relative strengths and weaknesses of companies that are acquisition candidates. Companies that rank the highest will be valued highly, while companies ranking below industry standards are likely to be eliminated from consideration or receive lowball offers. Whether you are a seller or buyer, the 17 factors will be useful in developing a strategic plan for your company that will increase its market value as a seller, or point you toward high-value targets as a buyer. In either case, allow at least a year to implement your strategic plan.

The 17 factors listed below fall into four categories: (1) financial factors, (2) customer and contract factors, (3) product and service offering factors, and (4) management and staffing factors. Contact Dick or Stuart if you would like help tailoring the 17 factors to suit the unique characteristics of your industry, or if you need guidance applying them to develop a strategic plan to help you achieve your objectives in the M&A market.

FINANCIAL FACTORS

1. Revenue Growth. Sustained year-over-year revenue growth is highly valued by potential acquirers, especially publicly-traded firms. A three-year Compound Annual Growth Rate (CAGR) in revenue of 15 percent or more is considered favorable in many industries. Higher CAGRs are frequently expected in technology-based businesses.

2. Overall Size. Bigger is definitely better in terms of sale price. Other factors being the same, a company with higher annual revenue is more attractive to buyers and will receive a higher multiple. Multiples range from 0.5 to 1.0 times annual revenue in most industries. The revenue multiple frequently is higher in product-based industries and specialty industries (e.g., companies with government security clearances).

3. Profits. Earnings before income taxes, depreciation, and amortization (EBITDA) is equal to revenue in determining the value of a company. EBITDA, which is a measure of pre-tax cash flow, multiples range from three times to eight times in most industries. The multiples could be higher in specialty industries and under unique circumstances (e.g., software products with high synergy to the buyer).

4. Meeting Projections. The ability to accurately project monthly sales, revenue, cost-of-sales, overhead expenses, and cash flow is attractive to potential buyers. Buyers value predictable performance, sound financial management practices, and a management team who understands the budget and consciously uses it in making everyday decisions.

5. Balance Sheet. Buyers are attracted to companies with adequate working capital, short cash cycles, a simple equity structure, and few (if any) contingent liabilities. A Current Ratio (Current Assets divided by Current Liabilities) of 1.5 is considered average in most industries.

6. Contingent Liabilities. Contingent liabilities, whether presented on or off the balance sheet, increase the risk of an acquisition and reduce a company's value. Eliminating or reducing contingent liabilities from the balance sheet (and notes to audited financial statements) is essential to reduce the buyer's risk in an acquisition.

CUSTOMER AND CONTRACT FACTORS

7. Customer Focus. Long-term relationships with customers who have firm budgets for future requirements are valued highly, especially when there are cross-selling opportunities for the buyers. Winning multiple projects from the same customers in the same line of business is preferred, as long as no single customer represents more than 30 percent of the annual revenue stream.

8. Customer Retention Record. A long history of winning consecutive contracts with the same customers adds value because it is interpreted as an indicator of customer loyalty and quality products and services.

9. Contract Backlog. A strong backlog of multi-year contracts/projects is valued highly by buyers. A contract backlog (un-invoiced balance on signed contracts divided by average monthly revenue) of more than six revenue months is considered good in most industries (does not apply to retail and other cash-basis businesses). Four to six months is average, and three months or less is viewed unfavorably.

10. Business Pipeline. A substantial number of bids submitted for high-value, high-probability contracts/projects with existing and new customers is valued highly. A pipeline with new business opportunities that exceed three times annual revenue (total of potential new contracts discounted for win probability) is considered good. Having a pipeline management process that accurately predicts future sales is valued highly by buyers.

11. Contract Vehicles. Indefinite Delivery/Indefinite Quantity (IDIQ) contracts and Basic Ordering Agreements (BOAs) with customers that can be used by the buyer for multiple purposes are valued highly.

12. Prime Contracts vs. Subcontracts. Direct customer relationships under prime contracts are much more highly valued than subcontracts. Generating more than 75 percent of annual revenue from prime contracts is considered favorable in most industries.

PRODUCT AND SERVICE OFFERING FACTORS

13. Business Focus. Having a recognized brand that produces: (a) a continuous stream of customers and sales, (b) a respected corporate reputation, and (c) substantial staff credentials and corporate awards in a few specialty areas is preferable to having customers scattered in widely diversified or unrelated areas.

14. Specialty Offerings. High-end products/services are valued more highly by buyers than administration or low-tech products/services because they tend to deliver higher margins and be more stable in difficult economic times. In addition, corporate characteristics that give a company a competitive advantage or form a barrier-to-entry for competitors are valued highly.

15. Intellectual Property. New technologies, patents, unique processes, software, websites, etc. and their proven ability to generate profitable revenue add significant value to a company.

MANAGEMENT AND STAFFING FACTORS

16. Management Team. An effective organization led by executives with proven ability, experience, and loyalty; and a well-understood vision of the company's strategic direction and succession plan are valued highly by buyers.

17. Staff Credentials. A staff with credentials recognized in the industry is highly desirable to buyers. For example, credentials include recognition as registered architect, Certified Public Accountant, Professional Engineer, government security clearances, and the like as appropriate to the industry. A better-than-industry-average employee retention rate is valued highly by buyers.

CONTACT THE AUTHORS

Dick and Stuart sincerely hope this book was interesting, insightful, and useful. If any "mistake" was especially valuable or inspiring, please let them know via e-mail at www.57expensivemistakes.com. They also would enjoy hearing about your adventures (or misadventures) in the exciting world of M&A transactions.

DICK STIEGLITZ, PhD

If you'd like help to groom your business to be sold, to prepare to buy another business, or to integrate an acquired business with yours, call Dick for consulting services. Send an e-mail with the basic information to dick@dick-stieglitz.com. He'll contact you to discuss the possibilities—the first consultation is always free. Dick is also available for workshops and keynote presentations about organizational change. Descriptions of his workshops and presentations are available at www.dickstieglitz.com. If you would like to read about changes in the business world, get a free subscription to Dick's monthly e-letter, *The Change Challenge*, at www.dragonsofchange.com.

STUART SORKIN, JD, LL.M, CPA

If you are ready to begin planning or negotiating to buy a company or to sell yours, contact Stuart for consulting services. Send an e-mail to Stuart at ssorkin@shspc.com and he will contact you to discuss your strategic options—the first consultation is always free. Stuart also is a frequent lecturer on legal and tax considerations in starting a business, growing and selling a business, and asset protection. Additional information is available at www. stuartsorkin.com.

ACKNOWLEDGMENTS

This book is the product of many relationships. While the interviews, writing, and editing required hundreds of hours, it was our relationships with CEOs, CFOs, CPAs, investment bankers, and attorneys who are actively engaged in buying and selling companies that made this book possible. We thank those generous men and women for providing fascinating M&A stories and valuable perspectives on the essential elements of success in M&A transactions. We especially thank them for their time and creativity, both of which are very precious indeed.

It's customary to acknowledge individual contributions from specific people. However, in this case, we must respect the requests of the M&A professionals who asked not to be named in order to protect their client's privacy. We felt that to name some contributors and omit others would not be fair, so we choose not to mention individual contributors. Except for publicly available information, we have not identified any participants in the M&A transactions and altered or omitted details that might identify the participants in private transactions. The fact that we can't acknowledge their contributions in no way diminishes our lasting appreciation for the treasured gift they gave us all by sharing M&A insights in a way that business owners can readily understand and use.

On the other hand, Dick and Stuart want to recognize the special contributions of three individuals who were instrumental in closing the sale of Dick's company: Jeff Houle, Managing Partner with Greenburg Taurig, LLP, who represented Dick's company; Chris Helmrath, Managing Director with SC&H Capital, who introduced Dick to the 17 factors that create value in a business; and Steve Pritchett, now with SC&H Capital, who worked tirelessly (sometimes at midnight) as Dick's investment banker until the transaction was closed. These three professionals—and friends—also provided guidance and inspiration for this book.

We also want to thank Pam Guerrieri of Proofed to Perfection, Patricia Bacall of *Bacall: Creative*, and our book shepherd Ellen Reid for their help in editing, design, layout, and printing this book. Their help enabled us to produce a professional book that we take pride in.

LIST OF ACRONYMS

ADD	Attention Deficit Disorder
AOP	Annual Operating Plan
ATM	Automated Teller Machine
BOA	Board of Advisors
BOD	Board of Directors
CAGR	Compound Annual Growth Rate
CEO	Chief Executive Officer
CFO	Chief Financial Officer
CMMI	Capability Maturity Model Integration
COO	Chief Operating Officer
CPA	Certified Public Accountant
CTO	Chief Technology Officer
CVE	Certified Valuation Expert
D&B	Dunn & Bradstreet
DNA	Deoxyribonucleic Acid
DOJ	Department of Justice
EBITDA	Earnings Before Income Tax, Depreciation & Amortization
ESOP	Employee Stock Ownership Plan
HR	Human Resources
IBM	International Business Machines Corporation
ICM	Integrated Change Management
IDIQ	Indefinite Delivery/Indefinite Quantity
IPO	Initial Public Offering
IRA	Individual Retirement Account
IRC	Internal Revenue Code
IRS	Internal Revenue Service
ISO	International Standards Organization
IT	Information Technology
JD	Jurist Doctor
LLC	Limited Liability Corporation
LL.M	Masters in Law
LOI	Letter of Intent

List of Acronyms, continued

M&A	Mergers & Acquisitions
MKP	The Mankind Project
NDA	Non-Disclosure Agreement
NOL	Net Operating Loss
PHD	Doctor of Philosophy
PM	Project Management
R&D	Research and Development
SAAS	Software As A Service
SBA	Small Business Administration
SDE	Seller's Discretionary Earnings
SEC	Securities & Exchange Commission
SWOT	Strengths, Weaknesses, Opportunities & Threats
TTM	Trailing Twelve Months
VP	Vice President

INDEX

57EXPENSIVEMISTAKES.COM